"The topic of this book might just be the most important one of all in terms of living a productive, joyous, and happy life. In this groundbreaking book, the author has provided us with a formula that absolutely guarantees the mastering of this-important trait. As one who has read countless books on person development - and learned tons from many of them - I rank this book as one of the most important ever! Buy a copy of this book for every-one you care about; it'll be the greatest gift you can give them. Learn these principles, teach them to your children, and teach them to the world."

- Bob Burg
Co-author of *The Go-Giver*,
Burg.com

"Kevin Clayson has given the world one of the simplest and most power-ful ways to change those obstacles into opportunities with FLIP the Grati-tude Switch. Everyone needs to read this book."

- Greg S. Reid
Author - Think and Grow Rich Series
KeynoteSpeaker.tv

"Kevin's energy is infectious, and you can feel his energy surging through-out FLIP the Gratitude Switch. Kevin was born to change lives, and his message is already doing just that. Kevin's FLIP formula is simply genius, and it WORKS!"

- John Lee Dumas, Founder and Host of Entrepreneur On Fire;
Bestselling Author of *The Freedom Journal*
EOFire.com

"I believe that Kevin has written the definitive 'gratitude how-to guide,' a timeless classic that is crucial to maximizing the quality of your life, the quality of your relationships, the growth of your business... and it's a book that the world has needed for a long time."

-Hal Elrod;
Author of *The Miracle Morning*
HalElrod.com

"Most of us (if not all) have big struggles that no one sees. Whether they be work issues, health issues, relationship issues, spiritual issues, or a combination, etc. FLIP The Gratitude Switch gives you a way to change your paradigm and find genuine peace and happiness while you are still knee or neck deep in the trial. I'm so grateful I am able to arm my kids with this arrow in their quiver while they are still young."

- Kelli Naylor
Homeschooling Mom of 4

"FLIP The Gratitude Switch is simply a MASTERPIECE! This is a book that every person should read and internalize. I've read many books and I expect this will become one of those books that goes down in history as a must read. What Kevin shares will help you change your life and see everything through a new and exciting lens. It will put you on the path to happiness and success with a simple formula that anyone can use. When you've finished the book, share it with your family and co-workers and help them experience the same transformation you'll experience!"

- Rob Shallenberger,
CEO of Becoming Your Best Global Leadership,
Former F-16 Pilot, and Bestselling Author
BecomingYourBest.com

"The principle of gratitude is quickly gaining support in the psychological literature as the starting point for every life improvement. Kevin Clayson understands this from a personal perspective in a way that is not only psychologically sound and accurate, but also refreshingly authentic and immediately applicable. Pay attention! He's reading the instructions to you. FLIP The Gratitude Switch is a quick peek into your own mind and something you can do today that will change the trajectory of every aspect of life."

- Paul H. Jenkins, Ph.D.,
Speaker, Author of *Positivity Psychologist*
DrPaulJenkins.com

"One of the reasons Rock Stars become legends is because they break the mold, and do something out of the ordinary. Kevin Clayson has done exactly that with his book FLIP The Gratitude Switch. There is no one out there saying the things Kevin is saying, and certainly not with the charisma and excitement he's saying them. I once told Kevin that he has that thing that makes someone stand out… in this book, that one thing is on full display. If you want your life to improve NOW, I highly recommend reading this book right away!"

- Craig Duswalt
Speaker, Author, Radio Host and Creator of *Rock Star Marketing*
CraigDuswalt.com

"As a Ghostwriter, I've written a lot of books (like, a lot), and I've never had one that's even come CLOSE to changing my life in the way that Kevin's has. You can ask my husband, my parents, and my kids… I'm a changed woman thanks to this book. And I'll always be grateful for Kevin and for the opportunity to work on this book that he poured his soul into."

- Jennifer Lill Brown,

TESTIMONIALS

Ghostwriter, Author, Freelance Writer, Book Guru
Homeschooling Mom of 3

"I couldn't put this book down. The principles Kevin teaches with regards to "FLIP" are true and correct. Thank you Kevin for putting your heart and soul into this book. This book will change lives if the principles are applied."

- David Keyser
Loss Prevention Manager
Father of 4

"I work full time and have 3 kids ages 11, 9 and 3 years. Life can get complicated and stressful, as it does for everyone, from work deadlines, long commutes, kids homework/school responsibilities, baby duties, supporting a marriage, home chores, etc. Patience can get thin and voices can get loud. I was generally happy, but sometimes wanted to be anywhere except for where I was. FLIPping the Gratitude Switch has made me enjoy the journey and focus on trying to live life in the now!"

- Amanda Dalnoki,
Mom of 3

"I thought I was good at being grateful. I've always been more optimistic than not, and never found it hard to be grateful for what I have, but, I now realized that I never really understood gratitude. I am amazed how powerful of an effect FLIPping the Gratitude Switch has. This book exceeded all the high expectations I had for it. Reading this book has been very thought provoking and an action inspiring experience."

- Al Harris,
Certified Financial Planner, CPA

"I love everything about this book. It's so brilliant. This book kept my attention the whole time. This message has already changed my life and my family's life and I intend on helping spread it as far as I can because it is so valuable and important. This message IS going to change so many lives! I am so honored to have had the privilege of reading this book. "

- Heather Brown
Stay-At-Home Mother of 3

"A golden book worthy of five stars - I have read a lot of motivational/self-help books, whether biographical or strictly motivational. Most of those books I've read from a high level. Those books are great, but at the end of the day all I can say is I feel better; my circumstances and life situations haven't changed. FLIP The Gratitude Switch is a very different book. This book and its simple formula changed my emotional state from frustration or anger to one of optimism and hope. Instead of reading FLIP

The Gratitude Switch as another motivational book that you put down and forget about among the other books, I challenge you to pick it up and implement the FLIP Formula in continuous daily practice. The more you use it, the more you'll notice changes in your life."

- David Kirlew
Graphic Designer

This book is 5 Stars for sure. I've already applied the FLIP quite a few times and it has really made an impact. Having kids with disabilities isn't an easy task, it is a TRUE blessing and I am so grateful for my little twin angels, the Lord knew I needed them, and being able to find the frustration then look for something good is something I'm always doing. Adding the other steps of Kevin's formula is taking things to a whole new level for me! This book is a game changer and life changing! I feel so blessed to have been able to read this book. It felt as if Kevin was personally there reading it to me."

- Michele Wright
Stay-At-Home Mother of 4

TESTIMONIALS

FLIP
the Gratitude
Switch

FLIP
the Gratitude
Switch

A Simple Formula To Change
The Trajectory Of Your Life

By
Kevin Clayson

All it takes is a single FLIP!

ISBN: 978-1537208244

Set in Book Antiqua
Cover Design and Interior Layout: Steve Airola, Mindslap, Inc
Editing: Jennifer Lill Brown

Dedication

This book is dedicated to the most important people in my life—my family. To my wife Malana, our three children—Brooklyn, Braxton, and Brody, and to Mom, Dad and Kristen, and Doug and Janet—I love you all. Thank you for loving me, but more importantly, thank you for letting me love you!

"To express gratitude is gracious and honorable,

To enact gratitude is generous and noble,

But to live with gratitude ever in our hearts is to touch heaven."

-Thomas S. Monson

Contents

PART I

The Red Door: A Story About the Path to Immeasurable Wealth

Part II

FLIPping Foundations

PART III
The FLIP Formula

PART IV
The Life of a FLIPper

Author's Note

I'm so thrilled you have this book in your hands; it is with tremendous care and careful dedication that I wrote these words. I wholeheartedly desire for the message in this book to shine a light on the increasingly dark places in this world, and on the dark places in the human experience. *The formula that has given me a _new life_ is contained in these pages.*

Why do I call it my *new life*? For many years, I suffered under the "poverty of endless discontentment," as David A. Bednar so eloquently put it. I was angry, entitled, unpleasant, and largely unhappy for a long time. Fortunately—and thanks to the fundamental philosophy contained in this book—I was able to break the shackles of depression, despair, and hopelessness and step into a life filled with joy, hope, and a *wealth of endless possibility.*

The process of writing this book has been a slow evolution. I have always tended to be a little (okay, a lot) thick-headed, and God has had to reinforce certain lessons time and time again before I finally receive them. But, He knew if He put the idea in my heart to write about these principles, then maybe, just maybe, the ideologies would finally take root in my life.

He was right (He always is). This book required me to learn and live these principles to such a degree that they will never leave my consciousness and certainly never be removed from my soul. The very creation of these words is a testament to the power of the principles contained herein. Before this book ever sells a single copy, this book has truly changed **MY** life.

I have watched this book change my wife's life. The principles brought her from a place of despair and borderline depression to one of such inspiration and hope, that she has gone on to work miracles in the lives of her friends and her family by helping them achieve goals they thought were impossible. This book would have never been written without her loving support and her example of these principles in action. I love you, Malana. I love you wholly, unconditionally, and completely.

This book was also written for my children. I wasn't sure what legacy I would leave behind for the world when I graduate Earth school and head back to my Creator one day, but I knew that I could control the kind of legacy I leave behind for my own children. I figured if I could teach my kids some of the things I learned the hard way, it might give them a jumpstart and fast track their ability to do good in this world—and it may infuse their life with more happiness in the process.

Brooklyn, Braxton, and Brody, I hope that something in this book, even if it is just one sentence, passage, or story, will impact your life in such a profound and eternally altering way that you may always smile more, feel more joy, and find the peace that only comes through living in that special place called *contentment*. I love you all wholly, unconditionally, and completely.

Now for you! I want to make you a promise. I feel confident making this promise because every person who has read about or heard me speak on the principles in this book and acted on them has been transformed in some way. I have researched, studied, and watched how the formula that you will be learning has a proven and profound impact on a person's happiness level. So now, here is my promise:

If you read this book and apply its principles, I guarantee with 100% certainty that it will increase your happiness, accelerate your success, and change the trajectory of your life!

In the pages that follow, you will read about my journey from being a miserable, entitled, selfish person to one that consciously chooses to utilize one simple tool, and how daily micro-decisions have changed the direction of my life. That's why I know it works. If you don't believe me, just read the book, put it to the test, prove to me that you have really tried to apply it, and if I'm wrong and it doesn't work, I will give you your money back. Deal?

With love and gratitude,

Kevin

Foreword

BY HAL ELROD
Author of the #1 bestselling book, *The Miracle Morning*
and Creator of *The Miracle Morning* Book Series

This foreword won't be short, because I want to give you some insight into the man who is about to radically transform your life, Mr. Kevin Clayson.

I first experienced the magic that is Kevin Clayson when I saw him perform a high energy rap performance, and dance routine, of the 90's hit song "Ice Ice Baby" by Vanilla Ice, at a mastermind in Los Angeles. No fear. No shame. All smiles and pure entertainment. I immediately loved this guy.

We were then serendipitously placed at the same table together, and since that first encounter, I have felt a kinship with him that has developed into a great friendship. We are both dedicated to changing the world with the messages we feel we have been given to share.

The message you're about to read in this book is one of the first things Kevin talked about at that mastermind, long before these words were even written. He lives it.

He leads by example and personifies his message in a way that draws people to him. As someone who considers himself a part of Kevin's **#gratifuel** movement, I can tell you that once you experience this message, it will leave an indelible mark on you, just like it has on me.

And it's already having a profound impact in the lives of the thousands of people who have experienced it through Kevin's keynote speeches, podcast appearances, or simply by knowing how he lives his life.

Story #1: How Kevin Saved My Favorite Tumbler
A few months ago, I was in Utah filming Kevin for *The Miracle Morning Movie*, a documentary about the power of morning rituals, based on my book. We filmed his morning gratitude routine at his home, with his wife and kids, and then we went to Kevin's office for a formal interview.

As I always do, I had my favorite Starbucks coffee tumbler with me (a special edition mug that they no longer sell), and I casually mentioned my love for the tumbler to Kevin.

After Kevin's segment, we left in a hurry to get to our next filming location about an hour away. Once we got there, I reached for my tumbler to refill it, only to discover that I had left it at Kevin's office. I called and asked him to ship it to me.

To my surprise, Kevin asked for the location of our current segment and insisted on driving the two-hour round trip just to bring me my tumbler because he knew how much I loved it.

The story may seem trivial to some, but to me it demonstrated how intensely Kevin is committed to his message and his mission to serve others. Kevin's willingness to serve taught me more about *FLIPping the Gratitude Switch* than words ever could.

I believe that Kevin has written the definitive "gratitude how-to guide," a timeless classic that is crucial to maximizing the quality of your life, the quality of your relationships, the growth of your business, and it's a book the world has needed for a long time.

Intellectual Gratitude vs. Soulful Gratitude

I feel so connected to Kevin and his message because I believe that the quality of our lives, at any given moment, is in direct proportion to the depth of gratitude that we are consciously present to. And there is a night-and-day difference between what I call "intellectual gratitude" and "soulful gratitude."

Everybody possesses intellectual gratitude — it's the type of gratitude that comes from our heads when we think about what we're grateful for, and is largely based on a programmed response. If I ask, "Are you grateful for your family?" you'd probably say, "Yes" without much thought, and the impact it had on you would be minimal.

Soulful gratitude, on the other hand, is the kind of depth, authentic, heartfelt gratitude that you feel intensely, that brings tears your eyes when you think about the people, and the life that you've been blessed with. Soulful gratitude is the key to unlock the door to a level of happiness and joy that few people ever experience. A level that we all deserve to feel, experience, and give to others every day.

Kevin has provided us with a path for stepping away from intellectual gratitude and into soulful gratitude. In this book, he shows you how to be truly grateful for all aspects of your life, including those that are difficult, and even painful, versus limiting your gratitude to only the good things in your life.

Story #2: How Gratitude Saved My Life

When I was 20 years old, my car was hit head on by a drunk driver at 70 miles per hour, and I was pronounced dead at the scene. Despite breaking 11 bones, being clinically dead for six minutes, spending six days in a coma, and being told I may never walk again, I realized that I could choose to be the most grateful I had ever been, even in the midst of the most difficult circumstances of my life. And that choice saved my life.

Kevin once asked me, "Hal, if you could put a finger on how gratitude specifically lifted you from your rock bottom, being found dead and told you would never walk again, to the massive success of changing millions of lives, how would you articulate that?" Upon reflection, I shared with Kevin what I will share with you here.

We all go through adversity, and that adversity is an asset if we choose to see it that way. For me, what gratitude — especially in the hospital—did for me is give me a new breath of life. In retrospect, I realize that even though I was facing a situation most people would consider horrible, I chose to view it as an opportunity. Gratitude was the key that unlocked the door to emotional well-being, enabling me to focus on what I wanted, as opposed to being stuck in what appeared to be my reality.

I remember telling my parents, "Look, if the doctors are right and I will never be able to walk again, I am going to be the most grateful person you've ever seen in a wheelchair, because I'm in a wheelchair either way, and I have that choice." Gratitude was the choice that saved my life, despite my circumstances. No matter what your wheelchair is, we all have that choice.

You hold in your hands the key to unlocking the power of gratitude in your life. I count myself fortunate to know Kevin, and that is why I am so grateful to be able to introduce you to Kevin, so that he can show you how to *FLIP The Gratitude Switch* in your own life.

Congratulations on beginning this journey.

With gratitude,

Hal Elrod
Author of *The Miracle Morning*
www.MiracleMorning.com

The Preface (You Don't Want To Skip)

Welcome to the party! I call it a *party*, because I truly feel that this book, and your experience while reading it, will feel like one giant celebration. It is a celebration of you; it is a celebration of truth; it is a celebration of life! Whether you bought this book, found it, borrowed it, or received it as a gift, the good news is that you now have it in your possession. So, take a moment and feel grateful that you have come into contact with something fresh and uplifting.

If you don't know what it takes to *FEEL* gratitude yet, don't worry. I will talk you through it, and soon, you will be the *Undisputed Heavyweight Gratitude Champion* of your life. For now, think about how great it is that you are able to read and learn new things. That is a type of gratitude you can already experience.

I've learned one overarching principle in this process: **Gratitude is a choice.** It is literally a choice you make to experience and interact with whatever life has in store for you. Don't buy into the lie that gratitude is a thing that *just happens.* It's time that people understand it is a thing you *make happen.*

You are powerless to change the past and you are powerless to control the future. The past was *then,* the future is over *there,* and you can affect neither of them in this moment. The only time that has any bearing on your life is the present.

Practice becoming present and waking up to feel the potential of each moment, because it is only in the NOW that you have power to affect the future.

Viktor E. Frankl, a holocaust survivor who wrote one of my favorite books called *Man's Search For Meaning,* put it this way, "Between stimulus and response there is a space. In that space is our power to choose our response. In our response lies our growth and our freedom."

As Frankl demonstrates, the idea that there is power in the present moment is not a novel idea; I didn't come up with that, however, the approach we will take to discussing it is new. I created this approach because when I was seeking ways to understand the concept of gratitude, I quickly discovered that it's one thing to say, "Be grateful," but it's another thing to learn how to <u>act</u> on that! *Consider this book your instruction manual on how to cultivate and activate gratitude in your life.*

There are plenty of books that can give you ideas for finding more happiness or fulfillment; there are lots of formulas for success. Each of them are useful, and each of them contains important truths. I've been reading personal development, self-help, and success books for years, and each has powerful truths and laws that, when applied, can chart a course for a better life.

As powerful and impactful as the quest for self-improvement has been in my life, I still felt like I was missing something. I found myself searching for one simple formula, process, or system that could instantaneously deliver happiness to me. That may sound like a lot to hope for, but I just *felt* the answer was out there — and in the process of writing this book, I found it.

One Single Word with Immense Power

I sometimes ask myself why it took the better part of 35 years to discover this powerful truth. I eventually realized that I couldn't find it sooner because, up until now, I wasn't *supposed* to know it completely — or perhaps I just wasn't ready. I had to embark on a journey of discovery that led me to its doorstep at just the right time.

Since this truth seemed so elusive to me, I could call this whole idea of applied gratitude a *secret* — but it is hardly a secret. In fact, it's an eternal and transcendent idea that has been around since the beginning of mankind, hiding in plain view. And, what happened to me after I made the discovery is what will likely happen to you — my brain was finally able to tune into the frequency of gratitude that has *always* existed.

I love the way Melody Beattie sums it up: *"Gratitude unlocks the fullness of life. It turns what we have into enough, and more. It turns denial into acceptance, chaos to order, and confusion to clarity. It can turn a meal into a feast, a house into a home, a stranger into a friend."*

Gratitude really is that powerful — and the absence of it is equally as formidable. WITHOUT gratitude, it doesn't matter whether you make $25,000 a year or $2,500,000 a year — it will never be enough. Without gratitude, the kids will always be too loud. Without gratitude, the checkout line will always be too slow. Without gratitude, traffic will always be terrible. Without gratitude, the movie theater popcorn will always be too expensive. Without gratitude, the weather will always be too hot, too cold, too wet, or too dry.

But WITH gratitude, you will be rich beyond earthly measure. With gratitude, the kids aren't too loud; they are just beautifully alive! With gratitude, the checkout line isn't too slow; you're just thankful you don't have to bag your own groceries. With gratitude, you're glad you have a car that runs. With gratitude, the butter on the popcorn and the person sitting next to you make it all worthwhile. With gratitude, the weather doesn't really matter — because you're breathing, and that makes it a great day!

Gratitude is a game changer. It can take the hour-long line at the DMV and turn it into the most interesting conversation with the person behind you that you've had in months. It can take that traffic jam and turn it into a powerful and life-altering time of self-improvement. The power of gratitude has had a profound and liberating effect on my life — and consequently on the lives of everyone I come into contact with — and it can do the same for you!

A Quick Vocabulary Lesson

The formula you will learn in this book is made up of a simple, four-step system that comprises what I call *FLIPping The Gratitude Switch*, with the letters F. L. I. P. each standing for a part of the FLIP Formula. It's a process that will enable you to understand, compartmentalize, and then *commoditize* the power of gratitude.

The FLIP Formula and its accompanying principles provide you with a way to turn gratitude into a *verb*—a daily action. They will provide you with the "fuel" you need to propel your life onward and upward. Gratitude can fuel life if you will let it; this is a principle you will learn as a part of the FLIP Formula called #Gratifuel.

Gratitude Fuel = Gratifuel

Notice the hashtag in front of *Gratifuel?* The hashtag is the marker of a movement that can collectively raise the levels of peace, happiness, and contentment if we are bold enough to share it. If you want to be part of the "GratiTeam" and join the crusade, post your transformative experiences with this book or the FLIP Formula on social media, along with the hashtag #gratifuel. That way, we can easily find each other and join forces to change our world for the better.

I believe that the practice of sharing is the fastest and most effective way to hold yourself accountable for applying the power of gratitude to your daily life. If you connect with me on social media, you will notice that I post my experiences regularly because sharing my #gratifuel experiences helps me stay committed to the biggest difference maker in my life—applying gratitude during life's most frustrating moments.

One Book, Four Distinct Parts

This book has been written in a unique way, one that I think you will really enjoy. I have found that everyone learns differently. Some of us want real life stories. Some of us want parables. Some of us just want the recipe, the steps, or the secret formula to create more ease and joy in our lives. Some of us want numbers, data, and analytics. I'm pleased to tell you that in this book, you will receive all of the above and more.

I've always been a fan of business parables, which is why I've included one in this book. *The Go-Giver* by Bob Burg and John David Mann is a book that has had perhaps the largest impact on my entire business formula, and my overall approach to life and people. I've also gained tremendous benefits from *3 Feet from Gold* by Greg S. Reid and Sharon Lechter, *The Greatest Salesman in the World* by Og Mandino, *Who Moved My Cheese* by Spencer Johnson, *The Goal* by Jeff Cox and Eliyahu Goldratt, and *The Energy Bus* by Jon Gordon. These are just a few examples of great lessons imparted through the art of storytelling.

When books teach powerful principles through stories, readers tend to more easily remember and implement those lessons. As a result, I felt inspired to write a story in the business parable format, and this parable comprises Part 1 of the book. The story is about a young man who is searching for answers to one of life's greatest mysteries. He finds an unexpected mentor who takes him on a journey of discovery and enlightenment that changes the course of the young man's life. The story will illuminate how gratitude is the single largest driver of success, and how feeling gratitude really is as simple as *flipping a switch.*

Parts 2 to 4 will have an entirely different feel. Part 2 is dedicated to sharing with you some of my story and examples from my real life of how I discovered the powerful FLIP formula. This formula has changed the entire trajectory of my life and sparked an international movement that is raising happiness and contentment levels across the globe, and I want you to know what brought me to the place in my life where I was compelled to discover it.

Part 3 will deliver the actual FLIP formula for cultivating and initiating active gratitude in your life and will demonstrate how every challenge, trial, and difficulty you face is the exact *blessing* you need at the exact time you receive it. Armed with this knowledge, you will discover that challenges and pitfalls become much easier to identify and navigate. You will see that each cloud in life not only has a silver lining, but is also waiting to rain blessings down upon you.

Part 4 has been designed as the exclamation point at the end of the sentence. You will fully understand the power and simplicity of the FLIP Formula and the power of active gratitude in your life by the time you finish Part 3; Part 4 will help you put it all into real life context.

Any single part of the book will give you tremendous value and nuggets of awesome, but I urge you to read the entire book. I want this message to take up residency in your soul, and reading the book in its entirety is the easiest way to ensure that will happen.

I've seen the ideas in this book impact people from all walks of life. They make sunsets more beautiful; they make happy moments even happier; they make your success level increase immediately; they have a positive impact on your bank account; they create joy from the ashes of despair.

One of the best quotes I've ever heard about gratitude is from a great man and religious leader named David A. Bednar. He said, *"The gift of Gratitude enables our appreciation for what we have to constrain desires for what we want. A grateful person is rich in contentment. An ungrateful person suffers in the poverty of endless discontentment."* I hope you will relate to, understand, and feel the power of those words by the time you finish this book.

The story you are about to read is about a young man who stumbled upon a wise mentor, a teacher who guides him on an adventure to find the most precious and powerful treasure on earth. Come along and read about a single night that changed everything—a night that would become the spark that changed the entire course of history.

PREFACE

PART I

The Red Door:
A Story About the Path
to Immeasurable Wealth

Chapter 1

Patros

Jacob had been wandering the city for hours looking for something. He didn't know what it was; he just wanted to find something special. The sun was just setting as he continued his quest for some unique, rare… *something*.

As the minutes ticked by, his surroundings became less and less familiar. *"What am I doing out here?"* Jacob pondered. *"And what do I think I'll find, exactly?"* As he questioned himself for the millionth time that evening, he stumbled upon an unmarked street. He looked down the narrow street and noticed flags and signs that appeared to be scripted in Chinese. *"I must be on the outskirts of Chinatown,"* he thought.

The street was quiet. There were a few small restaurants that undoubtedly served delicious dim sum, and a few tiny storefronts, the kind whose owners likely lived upstairs above their shops. The air was thick with the fragrance of incense wafting from the shops. A brief summer rain shower had covered the tinted sidewalk's surface with a shiny coating, adding to the beautiful sparkle of the mica crystals embedded in the concrete.

As he wandered aimlessly down the street, Jacob found himself falling into a routine that had recently become all consuming. He was once again pondering his life, considering the state of it, wondering what it was all for, and marveling that the culmination of a life's worth of experiences had led him to this night, in this city, on this sidewalk.

The warm air engulfed Jacob with feelings of optimism and anticipation. To most, it probably looked like just any other night in the city. But to Jacob, the night felt unusual… even extraordinary. He felt a sense of inevitability wash over him. He sensed he was on the brink of something life-changing, something spectacular. Now if only he could cross over and find it.

Jacob had been feeling this way for the past two years, but the feeling that something BIG was on the horizon had intensified in the past few weeks—almost like he'd been drifting toward the sun for years, and now he was nearing its surface. As he felt himself traveling down that familiar rabbit hole of introspection, he came to his senses and realized he was already halfway down the unmarked street.

As he approached a residence wedged in between two small shops, he heard an old man who was sitting out front cough loudly and clear his throat. Jacob turned to the old man and exclaimed, "God bless you, good fellow." He removed the pocket square from his suit coat jacket and offered it to the old man as a handkerchief.

As Jacob's eyes met the man's gaze, he realized that this man was not just old; he might be *ancient.* The old man's wrinkles were deep and many. There was a large grouping of especially deep wrinkles at the corners of his eyes. Jacob instantly realized why the wrinkles were so pronounced when the old man's face broke into an endearing smile of gratitude for the kind offering. They were *smile wrinkles.*

The man sat on a rickety stool in front of a brilliant and beautifully painted red door. A streetlamp perfectly illuminated the door, although the building itself was shrouded in darkness. The door's surface was delicately hand painted. Around the edges were gold leaf renderings of ancient dragons, the Chinese New Year kind. The interior of the door's surface was painted equally beautifully and contained, what looked to Jacob like a depiction of the story of a hero journeying through a treacherous land in search of great treasure. The artwork was so exquisite that it was hard to look away.

Jacob was jolted back to reality as the old man reached out his boney hand filled with years of accumulated liver spots to grab the kerchief from Jacob's outstretched grasp. Jacob wondered how many millions of smiles this ancient man had smiled in his surely 100 or more years. There was something compelling about him, and something even more compelling about that door.

The old man wiped the corners of his mouth and began to speak. His voice was feeble and meek, and yet there was a quiet, unmistakable power in it, as if each syllable was filled with a lifetime of accumulated wisdom.

"Hello there, Jacob. My name is Patros."

Still distracted by the beauty of the door, the young man briskly replied, "Nice to meet you. My name is… wait, how did you know my name?"

"Just a lucky guess, I suppose. I love that name. I had a son named Jacob, and you remind me of him. What do you think of my door?"

Jacob, in one excited, single breath, speed-talked a stream of consciousness as he blurted out his answer. "The door… well it's gorgeous. I'm at a loss for words. I mean, here I am in the city, just for the night, and something told me to go for a walk. I don't even know what I was looking for, but I felt like I should keep walking until I found it. This city is full of history and chaos, yet nothing has captured my attention like this door. And now, somehow, through a happy set of circumstances, here I am, standing before you and this… door. I must say, out of all of the architecture, museums, and sculptures in this busy city, I have seen nothing quite so interesting and beautiful as this conspicuous red door on this barely noticeable street."

He paused to take in the artwork and a deep breath before asking him, "Patros, is this your home? Did *YOU* paint this door?"

The old man's smile wrinkles appeared to deepen and widen as he said, "It is not my home, but I do own the contents of this building, and it was I who painted this door many, many years ago."

Jacob exclaimed, "YOU? Why, you must be an artist of some repute. This work is truly exquisite." He paused before continuing. "You say you own the contents of the building, but you do not live here." Another pregnant pause. "Where do you live?"

Patros' eyes briefly flitted towards the sky and just as quickly fell back to gaze upon the young man. "I live far from here, but I *do* consider this street home in a way. I spend many days here, many evenings, and I sleep just down the road from time to time when I'm in town."

Jacob scanned the old man, trying to mask his confusion and the hundreds of questions that came to mind for every one question Patros answered. Is this old man a traveler, a homeless man, or one of those simple, humble wealthy types? The old man's suit was impeccably tailored, but it carried many years of wear on its jacket sleeves. Patros did not appear to be starving or dirty, and he seemed to be quite spritely for his age. Jacob was impressed with this old man's goodly nature and again marveled at the quiet power he possessed.

Jacob wanted to question Patros about his life, about this door, and what lay behind the door. He opened his mouth to begin this incessant line of questioning, but thought better of it and instead chose to nod to the old man, and say, "Well then, thank you for allowing me to admire your beautiful door. I doubt I will ever forget it. I'll be on my way now. It's getting late, and I'm sure you would like to get some rest."

Jacob reached out his hand. Patros clasped his hand to return the gesture. Patros' hand, although boney and filled with signs of age, had incredibly soft skin. Jacob tried to politely break the grip, but Patros hung on. "Why leave so soon? You were kind enough to lend me your handkerchief and compliment my craftsmanship. I have offered nothing in return. Perhaps I can offer this. Would you like to see what's inside this door?"

Jacob's heart began to race with excitement—and a tinge of skepticism. This was, after all, a strange man in a strange city. They had just met, and Jacob did not know anything about him. But, like an uncontrollable itch that must be scratched, Jacob could not contain his eagerness and curiosity about the door and the contents that rest on the other side.

Against his better judgment, Jacob responded, "Perhaps, but first tell me—are the contents inside as beautiful as this door?"

Patros nodded and exclaimed, "More beautiful! But I must warn you, they are also more treacherous."

Jacob's skin tingled with curiosity. He felt a burst of excitement and uncertainty as he asked aloud, almost to himself, "What could *possibly* be in there?"

Patros' smile wrinkles deepened even further as he responded with a twinkle in his eye, "Adventure!"

Chapter 2

Adventure Awaits

At that moment, Patros' tone changed and he became somewhat solemn. He straightened and then leaned forward as he spoke. "My boy, it is no coincidence that you felt the desire to venture into the city tonight. It is no coincidence that you turned down this unmarked street. And it is certainly no coincidence that you are now standing in front of this door. I have beckoned you here. I am here this evening, for *you.*"

Here for me? What to make of such a cryptic statement? Jacob was taken aback. Could this be true? He had been feeling all night that something special was supposed to happen. Was this that *something?* Had he been summoned here? But, how? None of it made any sense.

"Patros, forgive me, but how could you summon me? You don't know me, and I certainly don't know you."

Patros acknowledged this statement with a flicker of a smile, "Yes, so you thought Jacob. But if I didn't know you, how did I know your name?"

"You said it was a lucky guess," replied Jacob, as both a statement and a question.

"My boy, I've known you your entire life. I've even walked with you on many occasions, although you did not know I accompanied you. I helped your parents raise you in a loving home; oftentimes, even they did not know I was with you.

"Every man has a destiny. Every person reaches a pivotal moment in his or her life, a moment that will change everything. That moment, for you, has come. All these years, I've been preparing you for this moment—and this door. It is true that I painted this door many, many years ago, and it is true that the story you perceived on its surface is a story about a young man, an adventure, and a treasure…"

Jacob's eyes opened wide. Had he told Patros what he thought the painting depicted? He knew he hadn't. "Patros, how did you know what I was thinking about the story depicted on the door?"

"I'm the one who gave you those thoughts."

Jacob thought in a stream of internal ramblings, "Who is this man? Shouldn't I be terrified, or at least suspicious, of his enigmatic words? Why do I feel I can trust him? Is he my guardian angel? He says he's been with me my whole life… Is he God?"

Patros was still speaking as Jacob's mind roared on with questions. He snapped back to Patros' words as the old man continued. "Jacob, I am here to present you with an offer. Are you ready to listen to this proposition?"

Jacob, mouth gaping open, nodded quickly in the affirmative.

"My boy, I have prepared a room inside this door to which I'm willing to grant you access. The room takes up the entirety of this city block. Located somewhere inside the room is a treasure chest full of immeasurable wealth, more wealth than you could ever spend in a lifetime, and frankly more than your children after you could spend in their lifetime.

"The key to the chest must also be located, but I will not reveal the location of the key or the treasure chest. It is up to you to seek and find both. You will need the key to open the chest. Your task is simple — locate the key, locate the chest, insert the key, and you will be granted access to immeasurable wealth."

Jacob became exhilarated at the thought of immeasurable wealth. "I'm ready, Patros! Let me in!"

Patros cautioned the young man not to be so hasty. "The task is not quite as simple as you may perceive. There is only one key, but there are ten different chests in the room. Each of the ten chests is crafted identically, but only one is red and gold like this door, and only one contains treasure of real worth. The other chests are equally heavy and are also beautifully crafted. However, they lack the vibrancy and color of the chest you seek — and they are filled with counterfeit treasure.

"Their contents will glitter, but beware, if you choose one of the nine counterfeit chests, the treasure inside will be nothing more than an echo of real wealth. It may fool the foolish; it can trick the weak-minded; but its contents cannot provide the immeasurable wealth you seek.

"You are welcome to choose any chest in the room — the key will fit them all — but the only way to gain access to the real treasure is to locate the red and gold chest and insert the key.

"I must also warn you, Jacob, that once you locate the key, you can only use the key to unlock a single chest. Choose correctly, and you get to keep all of the treasure the chest contains."

Jacob was swaying back and forth with excitement, his eyes looking upward, almost as though he was trying to convince his brain to memorize all the details. "Okay. Room… chest… red and gold… untold riches… key… counterfeit chests… I think I've got it."

But, Patros was not finished. "Before you decide to take me up on my offer, there are a few more details you'll want to hear."

"More details? What are they?" replied Jacob with minor annoyance.

"I understand your excitement, but many times, we rush into danger unprepared. I care for you too much to allow you to make that mistake."

"Yes, Patros, I get that, but… wait, did you say *danger?*"

Patros nodded. "The room is large, and it has been built to my unique specifications. You will find a special path on the floor marked by small golden tiles. Also located in the room are tremendous perils and danger. You will want to take care to avoid these."

Jacob's eyes became wider, and his heart began to beat a little faster.

"You will find other paths that contain very real and present dangers. Should you choose these, you may encounter moments of agonizing pain; you will stumble and fall; you may find yourself bruised, broken, and torn by what you encounter. If you allow yourself to be led astray from the true path to immeasurable wealth, you may find yourself at the bottom of a deep pit with walls too smooth to climb back out. You may find cliffs' edges that give way to deep and dangerous drop-offs. These dangers are some of the worst you may ever see. I promise you such paths are spotted with tragedy and loss."

Jacob unconsciously backed away from the door with a look of horror on his face.

"Jacob, I built this room many years ago, and few have ventured to enter. There have been some who let their haste dictate their path and have met their inevitable demise. I do not wish this for you, my boy. I've already told you how deeply I care for you. I cared for them too, but they could not listen to simple instructions.

"Do not follow in the footsteps of those who were distracted and arrogant in their ability to navigate the room successfully. Approach this room with humility, because what is contained inside can grant you a massive reward—or deliver inevitable destruction."

Jacob's confidence and excitement had now waned considerably. Still, the thought of immeasurable riches was enough to help him press on as he thought, *"It seems a little scary, but still easy enough. If I stay on the path, I will be able to find the key and the right chest. I can't imagine straying from the path for one moment knowing what harm could befall me if I do. I have confidence in the instructions Patros has given me. I can do this!"*

His resolve restored, Jacob said, "Patros, I truly believe what you have shared with me is true. I know I've been led to this point in time and directly to this place. I don't know if this is real or if I'm in a dream, but it all feels real… YOU feel real."

Jacob looked directly into Patros' bright blue eyes. If the eyes are the windows to the soul, the soul that resided behind Patros' eyes was full of wisdom, love, and tranquility. Jacob felt an indescribable feeling wash over his body, like someone had doused him with warm water that evaporated as it ran down his skin. That feeling… those eyes… this man…

"THIS IS RIGHT… THIS IS GOOD!" thought Jacob.

Jacob continued. "You probably already know, Patros, that I've been searching for the key to wealth. I've been reading and seeking incessantly, almost like I knew I had to prepare for this moment. And, now you have presented me with the opportunity to secure that wealth and discover that key. I am ready Patros. Is there anything else I need to know?"

Patros grinned widely. "Yes Jacob, and it is a good thing you asked.

I find it far too rare an occurrence for someone to question the reality with which they've been presented. Many simply become followers of their perceived reality, which is why only a few become influential leaders and innovators who faithfully and consistently strive for greatness and who question all things with boldness.

"It's been said that the opposite of courage in society is not cowardice; it's conformity. I have found this to be true. It requires great courage to question the status quo rather than to merely accept all that has been presented. You are proving once more Jacob, that perhaps I have truly built this room for YOU.

"However, there *is* one final condition I need to reveal. But, before I do, tell me, understanding the reward and the risks, are you willing to accept this challenge and perform the task I have laid before you?"

Jacob answered, quickly, and eagerly, "Yes!"

"Do you agree that this task has been communicated clearly and you understand what you are to do?" asked Patros.

"Yes."

"Will you enter this room, thereby entering into a contract that you agree to take on this task?"

Jacob took a deep breath as courage swelled in his breast, "I feel as though I was created for this task. Patros, I think this is my destiny. I still don't understand how I got here, yet I feel a calming reassurance that I am here for a purpose."

"So, is that a yes?"

"Patros, that is a *resounding* YES!"

The two men shook hands to make the agreement official.

"My dear boy, I can tell you with certainty that this IS your purpose. And now, here is the final detail. When you enter the room, it will be pitch black. I will not provide you with a flashlight, a lantern, or even a match. When you enter the room, you will be alone and must rely wholly on yourself, your intellect, and your abilities."

With that, Patros took out an antique looking key, inserted it into the keyhole, and turned the lock. Jacob heard a click, and Patros swung open the door to reveal what he sensed to be a large, cavernous, dark room beyond the threshold.

The light that had previously illuminated the ornamentation on the red and gold door now illuminated the first meter of a path tiled with small gold tiles. Jacob looked at the visible tiles, saw them trail off into the darkness, and he instinctively yanked the doorknob from Patros' hand and slammed the door in front of them. No way was he going to step into total darkness.

Jacob started questioning everything. Had he just walked into some serial killer's diabolical game? Why didn't Patros reveal until after their agreement that the room would be blanketed in total darkness? Why did he make Jacob commit to the task before that vital piece of information was shared?

Enveloped in frustration and growing anger, Jacob took a step away from Patros. "What is this? What are you? You had me thinking that after tonight, I would possess wealth and fulfillment, but all you wanted to do was lure me in for some twisted game?"

Patros was unmoved. "No Jacob, everything I have told you has been orchestrated for your benefit, not your destruction. You can enter this room and choose failure, pain, frustration, and ultimately death; or you can enter this room with your unwavering commitment and faith that all will be well, and you will succeed."

"How can that be possible?" retorted Jacob. "There is no light. I can't see the gold tiles that are supposed to lead me to the key and to the right chest — the same gold tiles that are supposed to keep me out of harm's way. If I can't see the path, how will I know if I'm nearing danger or headed in the right direction?

"It sounds to me like failure is inevitable. I will probably fall into some dark abyss. Even if I **do** manage, by some miracle, to stay unharmed, how can I find the key? Even if I could somehow manage to not die, find the key, and stumble upon a chest, there is only a ten percent chance the chest I pick will be the right one. If I pick the wrong one, I will ensure my failure. No wonder so many others have perished. How could they possibly succeed? How could I possibly succeed?"

Tears began to well up in Jacob's eyes. He felt betrayed and deflated. And yet, Jacob could not bring himself to break eye contact with Patros and could not bear to walk away.

With strength and compassion, Patros replied, "Jacob, what you fail to realize is that while many have tried and failed, many have also tried and succeeded. You are asking the right question: '**_How_** could I possibly **_succeed?_**' But, you are not asking it the right way. Perhaps the emphasis should be on another word, as in, 'How could I **_possibly_** succeed?' In short, why have you not asked me, 'How **_can_** I succeed at this task?'"

The old man's wisdom struck Jacob right between the eyes. Jacob was viewing the task and the conditions as absolute, but what if he was simply missing an important detail? Jacob recalled the old man's words: "_The room is large, and it has been built to my unique specifications. You will find a special path on the floor marked by small golden tiles._" Why would Patros take such care to tile the floor with gold tiles if they would never be seen? He continued questioning out loud, "What would be the point of having the path if its guidance was rendered useless by the darkness in the room?"

Patros had also said he would give Jacob no light whatsoever upon his entrance to the room. Jacob thought, "_Just because he won't **give** me light doesn't mean there won't be some **way** to illuminate my path. Maybe all I need to do is figure out how to **find light.**_"

"Patros, is there light that is available to me once I'm in the room?"
Patros slowly nodded his head in the affirmative.
"Is there an easy way for me to receive or locate the light?"
Again, an affirmative nod.

"Patros, will you tell me how I can find the light?"

"Now you have discovered it, Jacob. The power is within you to find the light that will illuminate the path and make your success inevitable. The room is large, the chest you seek is somewhere in the room, and there is a path of golden tiles that will lead you directly to it. If the room is filled with light, you will clearly see the many paths and perils that will keep you from your goal and you will see that there are ten chests in the room. **I am not providing light for you, but I am not preventing you from receiving and using light as a part of your task.** Once you cross the threshold, reach your left hand out and feel the wall, just inside the doorframe, exactly at your shoulder's height, and you will feel a light switch. **Simply flip that switch, and all will be illuminated. The room will be flooded with bright and brilliant light!"**

"I knew it!" exclaimed Jacob.

With caution in his voice, Patros added, "Let me be clear Jacob. It is *your* choice to perform the task in the dark, or to flip the switch and perform the task in the light. If you choose to find and flip the switch, the path will be illuminated, the dangers will be easy to navigate, the key will be easy to find, and the right chest will be easy to spot—and you will inevitably become immeasurably wealthy.

"Your success in this adventure is a choice. You will, however, find that it is easy to sabotage your success in the room if you choose to proceed in total darkness. Do you understand?"

"Yes, of course. Although I possess the tools and knowledge to succeed, I can still choose failure. Is that right?"

"Yes, Jacob! Are you ready?"

Jacob nodded, and on cue, as Patros had done before, he pulled the old metal key from his pocket, inserted it into the lock, and turned it with a loud click. Once again the beautiful red and gold door swung open to reveal the dark and cavernous space inside.

Jacob and Patros exchanged glances of joy. "Good luck, my boy."

Jacob took a step inside the door, reached to the left, found the switch, and gave it a single flip. With that small simple act, the room began flooding with brilliant light as Patros extended his hand to grasp Jacob's shoulder.

"Jacob, you will need this." Patros handed him the key. "I told you that if you chose to flip the switch, it would be simple to locate the key. You have chosen to flip the switch; here is your key."

Jacob turned to face his task; a task that he immediately realized would not be quite as simple as he thought. Jacob was shocked to see what lay in front of him as the room slowly illuminated.

Chapter 3

The Treasure Room

Jacob turned to face the interior of the cavernous room, as row after row of lights powered on. As the room grew brighter, he could easily see the path directly before him. He waited for his eyes to adjust as the room glowed with its startlingly brilliant light—and what he saw astonished him.

This was the largest room he'd ever seen. It was bright and vibrant once all the lights were on, but there was a calming simplicity to the space. Jacob cast his eyes around to see if he could catch a glimpse of all the perils and dangers Patros had spoken of, but there was nothing to see—just an empty, large room. Directly in front of him, at least a hundred or more yards away, he saw something glimmer in the light. Even from far away, he knew what it was. It was the chest. The key warmed in his hand as he thought of the treasure that waited.

The chest appeared to be located at the very end of the gold tiled path in the center of the room. Even from far away, the chest had an illuminating quality, no doubt aided by the spotlight hanging far above that caused the gold flecks painted on top to dance, almost as though the chest itself were alive. There were a grouping of items flanking the red and gold chest, but the chest glowed so brightly, it was hard for Jacob to make out what might be surrounding it.

He began slowly walking down the path, but the walking only lasted a few paces before he began jogging. The jogging did not last long either. Twenty feet inside the door, Jacob had broken into a sprint down the gold tiled path, anxious to capture his prize.

Breathless as he ran towards his goal, he saw that there *were* in fact other, darker treasure chests neighboring the red and gold chest.

"Those must be the counterfeit chests!" he exclaimed, his words echoing through the vacant space. He continued to run, curious about why the other chests were placed so closely to the red and gold chest.

After what seemed like a small eternity in Jacob's life, he finally arrived at the precious red and gold box. His lungs heaving, and with a slight trickle of sweat developing on his brow, he took a deep breath. There it was—the very chest that was supposed to contain immeasurable wealth.

It was exquisite and much larger than Jacob had expected. It must have been at least five feet wide, three feet deep, and five feet tall. It had been crafted from a single piece of wood, and done so with tremendous skill and care. *"Yet another shining example of Patros' handiwork,"* Jacob thought. The only cuts in the wood were where the hinges were installed to allow the top of the chest to open.

On top of the chest was the same painting Jacob had seen on the door. It depicted the hero overcoming challenges on his journey to arrive at a great treasure. The sides, front, and back of the chest had been painted the same red as the door, and the identical gold leaf painting style framed each of the visible panels that had been carved into the wood. Located on the front of the chest was a keyhole that looked just like the one on the red door that led to this strange room.

Jacob stared at the chest, feeling that all of life's questions were about to be answered. He had this odd feeling that after years of working hard, serving others, and providing value to his customers, his employers, his employees, and humankind in general was all about to pay off. He felt like every good deed he'd ever done had somehow been responsible for laying those small gold tiles on the path that led him to *this* spot, in front of *this* chest, at *this* moment.

He paused, savoring the victory of what he perceived as arrival. *"I did it! I've made it! I have the key, I'm going to unlock this chest, and I'll never have to work another day of my life… I am about to become immeasurably wealthy."*

He envisioned the volume of precious metals and jewels that must be waiting for him in that chest. More than his brain could fathom, he imagined. Or maybe it was one massive diamond, bigger than the world had ever seen. What could it be? Jacob was almost blinded by the possibilities. His vision narrowed, and all he could see was this chest—his prize—and the key to becoming immeasurably wealthy.

He stole a glance down at his feet and the golden tiles that lay below. He noticed that the gold tiles extended further out than he expected. The gold tiles widened to encompass all of the other 9 counterfeit chests that each had been placed on either side of his red and gold chest.

The thoughts of the colossal diamond and unlimited gold left his mind, and confusion entered in their place. "How could this be?" He pondered aloud. "I thought the pathway was only supposed to lead me to *my* prize. How can the tiles also lead to these other chests?"

In his excitement, he had failed to notice that the tiled path had fanned out about twenty feet before he reached the chest. As he stared at the other golden paths, something else caught his eye. The chest on the far left… it was open. Even more fascinating, there was something glimmering inside.

The chest stood of equal size and beauty to the red and gold chest, with its top unlocked and opened, leaving about a three-inch gap. "Patros said I can only use the key on one chest, but I don't have to use the key on that one. It's already open," he said. "Besides, it is located inside the gold path, so it must be fine to go take a peek."

He glanced back at the red and gold chest and decided it was not going anywhere. Jacob followed the gold tiles right up to the open chest. He flung open the top and saw it was almost overflowing with gold and other precious things. "But didn't Patros say that what was in these chests was counterfeit? Didn't he say something like, 'Their contents will glitter, but beware, if you choose one of the nine counterfeit chests, the treasure inside is nothing more than an echo of real wealth?"

Jacob turned it over in his mind, "None of this *looks* fake to me."

He dove his hands into the chest to feel its contents. Jacob's hands did not enter easily, as the gold coins were immensely heavy. He knew gold was supposed to be heavy, but how could he really tell if the contents were real? He picked up a beautifully minted gold coin and held the heavy round currency in his hand. Thanks to watching too many cartoons and pirate adventure movies, he bit into the coin, not sure what that was supposed to indicate. It didn't seem to give. Does that mean it's fake or real? Gold is supposed to be soft, right?

"Well, not necessarily," thought Jacob. He had recently been researching whether or not to invest in gold, and he read that gold coins with as much as .9999 purity might be mixed with alloy so that they weren't too soft. Thus, the lack of give didn't necessarily mean it wasn't real gold.

There was no taste to it; it didn't have that metallic hint you get if you've ever been dumb enough to put a penny in your mouth. So, maybe that meant it was real?

He picked up a gold bar, maybe seven inches long. It was heavy, perhaps 10 or 20 lbs. "Gold is heavy," he thought. "This sure does *seem* real."

He remembered hearing once that real gold would be stamped with an indicator of its purity. He turned it over in his hands. On the bottom was a small stamp that said "24K."

The coin *felt* like a gold coin and *looked* like a real cold coin, and then there was the bar. The bar was heavy. It *looked* like a real gold bar, and it had the stamp, too. He began to think that it *must* be real gold.

He turned his attention to the diamonds. He picked up one of the large diamonds and pretended to examine it, as if he knew what he was looking for. He'd read somewhere that if you try to fog a diamond with your breath, like you would a mirror, that a real diamond quickly disperses the heat and doesn't stay fogged.

He blew his warm breath onto the surface, and the fog dispersed almost immediately. This was real! It was all real, all of this treasure was REAL... it had to be!!

Jacob again grew confused. If the other nine chests are full of this kind of treasure, what could his red and gold chest possibly be filled with?

He started to head back to the red and gold chest, but as he took a step—almost like he'd triggered it—the other eight chests sprung open to reveal their equally impressive and dazzling contents. Each of them was also squarely sitting along the gold tiled path.

Jacob performed a few quick tests on the diamonds and gold in the other chests. All of it *appeared* to be real. How could the contents of the red and gold chest be worth more than what was already in front of him? All the chests were open and available. Couldn't he take the contents of each one? Even a handful or two would surely be worth millions of dollars.

He looked down at the key in his hand. He glanced at the red and gold chest at the end of the golden tiled path. He gazed upon the precious metals and stones in the "counterfeit" boxes.

He started to wonder if this was part of the game. Was he actually supposed to pick the nine other chests? Were those the real prize? Maybe Patros intentionally left out some vital piece of information like he did with the light switch in order to impart a lesson.

"At a minimum, I know Patros wants me to succeed, and he wouldn't lie to me just for a game… so, there *has* to be a reason for all this. But then again, where are all of the pitfalls and potential harm Patros warned me about?" Jacob looked around the massive room and couldn't see anything harmful or even slightly ominous.

He again thought of the words of Patros. "Located in the room are tremendous perils and danger. You will want to take care to avoid these."

Had he ever explicitly said there would be a booby trap or sharp spikes? No, he didn't. He had said things like, "In this room there will be many ways to injure yourself and cause yourself harm." Jacob realized that he had let his imagination run wild. Those words didn't have to mean there would be alligator pits or blades swinging from the ceiling.

Jacob began to comprehend Patros' game. Everything Patros said had a purpose, but it didn't mean the words were literal. "He did say something about being at the bottom of some pit or falling off a cliff. But, what if he meant it metaphorically?" Jacob thought.

Something inside Jacob stirred. He knew he was missing *something*.

He turned his attention back to the chests and again found himself replaying the words of Patros. "Located somewhere inside this room is a treasure chest full of immeasurable wealth. In the chest is more wealth than you can ever spend in a lifetime, and frankly more than your children after you could spend in their lifetime."

Jacob looked again at the chests full of precious things. "That is a lot of money, to be sure, but between my children and I, if we were reckless, I'm certain we could spend it all. Plus, how can these nine chests be 'immeasurable wealth?' I could get the contents appraised and know exactly how much I had."

A thought occurred to Jacob. "Wait! Maybe these chests *are* the peril. They are on the path, but maybe that's because I'm supposed to encounter them and choose to avoid them. What if their treasure is cursed? What if choosing those chests dooms me to some wretched existence?"

It was all beginning to click. Again, the words of Patros reverberated through his head. He felt like he was on to something, "In the chest is more wealth than you can ever spend in a lifetime…"

"Patros said 'CHEST'… singular. That means it can't be these nine, or he would have said chests."

If anything, Patros was certainly deliberate in his language, and Jacob had the feeling that every word Patros uttered had been laced with specific purpose and meaning, but his young mind could not possibly understand its full meaning—at least not yet.

One chest. Immeasurable Wealth. It had to be the red and gold chest.

He approached the red and gold chest once again. The time had come. He inserted the key Patros had given him and lifted the heavy lid, swinging it backwards to give him access to the chamber within.

The inside of the chest was shadowed. In fact, he could catch no glimpse of any treasure whatsoever. It appeared to be… empty.

He stuck his head in the chest trying to figure out what he was missing. Was there another step? Was this some sort of elaborate scavenger hunt, and this was just the first of the clues?

Patros said the chest contained "immeasurable wealth."

So, where is it?

Jacob plunged his head farther into the box and saw nothing. He reached a hand inside and began running it along the sides of the chest, and moving his hand back and forth inside the chest, through the air, hoping that his hand would hit something. He began frantically swabbing the inside of the chest with his hand, reaching further down with each swab—and then his finger touched something.

What was that? He leaned further into the chest and his heels came off the ground, his toes the only things still anchoring him. He still could not reach the bottom, and so he gave in and let his feet detach from the ground.

As his waist teetered on the edge of the chest, he reached as far as he could, and then… there, he could reach it. He picked up the small role of parchment between his thumb and forefinger and pulled it upward, shifting his weight back to his feet, as he stood straight.

He held a small piece of rolled parchment that was tied with golden string. Jacob delicately untied the string and unrolled the parchment. The parchment felt so old that Jacob was worried it would fall apart. His eyes scanned a letter that seemed quite long. He carefully scanned down to the final paragraph, and just below it was a beautifully signed name at the very bottom.

It was a personalized letter to Jacob from Patros. Jacob snapped his head back towards the door. "Patros! Are you in here? What is this?"

His voice echoed and bounced off the concrete walls surrounding him, and then the sound waves diminished in intensity, and Jacob's echo disappeared.

He was alone.

Chapter 4

The Letter

Settling back into his solitude amidst the expanse of the room, his eyes became fixed on the beautiful handwriting of Patros, and he began to read the letter out loud:

My Dearest Jacob,

If you are reading this, it means you flipped the light switch to illuminate your task, thought carefully about my words, chose not to take what was offered in the other chests, and opted instead to find the immeasurable wealth promised in this one. *Congratulations, my boy. You have completed your task!*

You may be wondering how this chest can possibly contain immeasurable wealth when all that is here is this letter. All will be made clear soon enough, because in this letter, you will find the world's most powerful truth, and quite possibly, its best-kept secret. But, before I share the secret, I want to explain why I didn't give this letter to you when we first met on the street.

If I had simply handed you this information, it would have been too easy to forget. It means far more to learn from experience than from words, and even more to learn from *application*. By creating this room and a series of tasks for you, once you receive this truth, you will never forget it. Resolve now to take this secret and act on it, and the wealth you receive can never be fully spent, extinguished, or forgotten.

Jacob, you have a great work to do. You have been called to bless the human family and reveal this secret to as many of them as possible. As you teach this secret, earthly riches will be yours, but more importantly, the wisdom of the ages will be unlocked, and you will have limitless wealth in mind and spirit. *What you can come to possess as a result will dwarf what is contained in the nine other chests.*

The chests of gold and jewels can buy you a measure of happiness in this world, but none of it is transferrable when you leave the earth. The secret contained within this letter will make you immeasurably wealthy on this earth AND in the next phase of your existence, the bounds of which are limitless and cannot be measured by earthly reckoning.

I want you to be committed to your success, but with the simple understanding that your success is inextricably intertwined with how abundantly you place other people's interests before your own. That is why you must have a singular focus on sharing this secret once it is revealed. More importantly, LIVE this secret and allow it to take up residence in your soul. Breathe it in, and let it fuel your life!

My son, while the key to immeasurable wealth is now in your hands, the secret is meaningless if you don't understand the conditions in which the immeasurable wealth must be obtained, and if you don't understand the importance of it. This entire experience is meant to serve as a metaphor for your life—and you should share this metaphor, as part of your life's work, to reveal the secret to all who will listen.

This room is a symbol for your life. You are in the room, just as you are in life at this moment. You were tasked to successfully navigate the room while looking for something that will satisfy the need to find what you probably perceived as *physical* treasure. Just as in life, many people spend most of their time seeking that thing they believe will satisfy. Some find it; far too many do not.

Each person has a specific set of abilities and a unique gift. Yet, so many of them seek to find some new gift, while rarely acknowledging the one they've already been given. This adventure was designed to help you see the gift you were already given, a gift that was given from the moment you came into this world, which is simply this:

You have the exclusive power to CHOOSE to make yourself happy.

Next to the bestowal of life itself, the right to direct your life is one of the greatest gifts you will ever receive. No earthly treasure can fulfill the way this eternal one can.

Now, if I had offered you the opportunity to enter the room as a way to find "happiness," how quickly would you have dismissed my offer or considered it a hoax? However, by offering an "adventure" and the promise of a treasure hunt, how much more likely was an adventurous and daring soul like yours to accept my offer? You chose adventure, and now I will reveal the treasure at the end of your quest:

Immeasurable Wealth, in this life and in the life to come,
is TRUE HAPPINESS.

But, there is more to understand, so much more. Just as this room is a symbol for your life, every piece of your experience this evening is also a symbol for something you have encountered or will encounter in what can be a dark and dreary world.

The golden tiles are symbols for the choices you make. If you are consistently living your life based on solid, truth-driven principles, those good choices compound and forms a path that leads you to genuine and everlasting happiness. Being kind, caring for those in need, working hard, loving your family, serving others, and having humility are just a few of the decisions you have made that have created the path you now stand on, the path that has guided you to the ultimate treasure.

The nine chests are symbols for temporary happiness. Outside this room, even as you walk the golden tiled path of your real life by sticking to the principles you know to be true and right, you will still encounter counterfeit happiness. This is inevitable. No matter how righteous you attempt to be, counterfeit happiness is always no more than a step away — and it will always appear to be instantly accessible and glistening with the shiny promise of a better life.

True happiness, however, is the kind that keeps you afloat no matter how hard the storms of life try to drown you. True happiness is the kind that fulfills you and allows you to be rich in contentment. Temporary or counterfeit happiness is the kind that will never fully satisfy, and it will lead to a life of suffering from the poverty of endless discontentment.

Counterfeit happiness comes in many forms — it can be represented by alcohol, drugs, promiscuity, immediate gratification, greed, fame, an abundance of unhealthy, rich food, and much more. Such things represent a form of pleasure to many, but none of them have the ability to create authentic, lasting happiness. When counterfeit happiness passes through the system, it leaves a hole that needs to be filled by more of the things that will leave you even emptier than before… and destroy you in the end.

It has been said that anything worth having is worth working for, and yet the world betrays this adage with an endless array of ways to immediately experience some morsel of fleeting happiness. True happiness — eternal, perfect happiness — must be won and earned. It must be purchased with time and with dedication. It cannot be temporarily leased.

Think of how many people have spent a lifetime trying to attain a small portion of what is in any one of those nine chests you forfeited. And yet, no matter how much money they have, they constantly live with the fear that what they have isn't enough. The more happiness they seek through acquiring fame and fortune, the more it escapes through their fingers like smoke.

That is why the nine chests were found along the path — to remind you that while your path may be true, you will always be met with choices that can lead to destruction. You must be vigilant and use the path you are on only to obtain real, fulfilling wealth and happiness.

The cliffs and pitfalls I spoke of are symbols for the hardships of life. I am sure you noticed that there were no physical dangers visible in the room. That is because you can meet your demise in this room without the presence of an alligator pit or rocky cliff. What if you chose to stray from the golden path and spend the remainder of your days wandering the room's expanse, constantly muttering about your lack, never choosing to see what is actually in front of you? What if you decided the game was rigged, and you were doomed to failure?

You are welcome to leave this room with or without your treasure;

23

you are welcome to wander and express discontent for the rest of your days; you are even welcome to take up your treasure and keep it to yourself, self-ishly hoarding what could be shared with the world. Each outcome is possi-ble, and each one is rooted in that precious gift you have — the gift of choice.

Many people will wander the room of life with no clear picture of purpose or possibility. It would feel as though you were wandering this room in the dark, always searching, never finding. What would the mind do if it felt it had no options and no way to succeed? Would that not lead to assured destruction?

A series of poor choices can become deep chasms from which you may not be able to escape. All of them lead to assured destruction, and all of them prevent you from experiencing the fulfillment you seek. The pits and the cliffs of life are the hardships, the difficulties, the tragedies, the failures, and the storms that inevitably will rage.

Life's pitfalls are always present, even while on the path. But, while you are always faced with their reality, you are never required to give into their tricks or let them defeat you. You are not required to stray from the path; straying is a *choice*. You are not required to let life's pitfalls destroy you; you *choose* to give them power. You will be constantly assaulted by the world's many difficulties and trials. Should you choose to submit, you will never find the immeasurable wealth you seek.

You have the gift of choice. You may choose to aimlessly wander to your detriment and destruction. You may choose to take up the earthly trea-sure and wander with it in your grasp, but never able to use it. Or you may choose the path I've provided, a path that will also serve as your guide out of this room and back into the world where you can use the power of choice and share the immeasurable wealth, thus multiplying your gifts.

The key I gave you is a symbol for knowledge. It is something that can be obtained but will be useless if not applied and used in the right way. You knew the red and gold chest contained immeasurable wealth, but you had to choose to use that knowledge as you chose to use the key to unlock it.

And now, my boy, we have come to the singular, central principle of this entire event — and that is the light and how you accessed it. The light that you need to illuminate the path, the light that shines on the red and gold chest, the light that can illuminate the pitfalls and the counterfeit treasure…

What does this light represent?

When you thought you would have to navigate the room in the dark, you felt the absence of light even before you attempted the task. You likely, in equal measure, felt the desire to have the light. You didn't know how to introduce light into the room, but you knew that without that light, the task was impossible. With the light, however, the task became feasible. With the light on, you felt certain you could succeed.

What would it be like to always feel that we had light available to us in unlimited supply? What would it feel like to know that the accessible light

24

would allow us to successfully navigate any challenge or task, whereas in the darkness, those same challenges and tasks may seem impossible? Jacob, you already possess that light in your life.

The light that will illuminate your life is GRATITUDE! Gratitude is the ONLY thing that can lead you to unlimited and unrestrained happiness and thus, immeasurable wealth.

Here is how it all connects. Without light, only darkness remains—and darkness is *fear*. If only fear is present, there can be no *hope*. If there is no hope, there is only *despair*. If there is only despair, there can be no *purpose*. Without purpose, there is no *meaning*. Without meaning, there is no *life*.

Happiness, then, is the meaning of life, and a life full of meaning enjoys the blessing of *eternal existence*. The purpose of eternal existence is to have unlimited *joy*. Joy only comes through being rich in *contentment*—and finally, contentment is only found through the eternal power of *Gratitude*.

The existence of Gratitude will constantly illuminate life and all of its challenges, pitfalls, and failures, as well as its joys and triumphs. Not only will gratitude allow that which is beautiful to become more beautiful, but the power of gratitude will also illuminate each of life's challenges and allow you to see the beauty in them.

There is success embedded in every failure.
Without gratitude, failure is nothing more than disappointment.

There is joy embedded in despair.
Without gratitude, despair is nothing more than a hole left unfilled.

There is hope embedded in tragedy.
Without gratitude, tragedy is nothing more than loss of hope.

There is healing embedded in pain.
Without gratitude, pain is simply unnecessary.

There is a new beginning embedded in every ending.
Without gratitude, endings are always final.

This is the immeasurable wealth you have now come to possess, and that you are now charged to share with the world. But, before you can begin receiving the eternal wealth of this knowledge and your earthly rewards as well, there is one final integral component that you must understand. *How did you access the light?* What is the simple thing you did in order to receive the very light that is currently allowing you to access the eternal truths you are now reading?

It was your decision to turn on the light. You CHOSE to flip the switch.

The simple act of flipping that switch is the key to it all.

25

Even after I told you there was a way to have light in the room, you still had to *choose* to flip the switch. Most people don't ask the right question as you did, and they go through life unaware that the switch that will reveal their path is but an arm's reach away. Even more tragically, others are aware of this simple truth, but choose not to flip the switch.

You were aware of the switch's existence, but it still required some level of faith in my words that flipping the switch would be the answer. Faith in my words wasn't enough; what it took in the end was conscious action.

I could have told you of the switch before you questioned me. I could have told you that by simply flipping it, you could access all the light necessary to complete your task. But even if you believed me, had you not made the conscious decision to flip the switch, you never would have been given access to the light.

In this room, it was the simple act of flipping the switch that made everything possible. The light allows you to navigate every pitfall, illuminate the path, obtain the key, find the treasure, and significantly improve your chances for success.

Without light, the task of finding immeasurable wealth is impossible.

You are now aware that the power of gratitude will illuminate all of life's challenges and allow you to successfully navigate anything that may come your way, but that light will be unavailable to you if you don't make the mindful, daily decision to flip your *Gratitude Switch* in order to access the light. Think of the flipping of the switch as the simple act of choosing to consciously express, feel, and experience gratitude no matter what life may throw at you.

You must flip your Gratitude Switch daily, hourly, even by the minute, if necessary. When you leave this room, the weight of the world and its darkness will once again rest upon you. Out there, few people know that the key to happiness, peace, and fulfillment is within them. They do not know that a daily choice to flip an internal switch is the key to unlimited happiness. That is why you must tell them.

If they do not know about the switch, they will continue to wander through the darkness of life searching for some kind of light. They may stumble upon and access the counterfeit treasures, those things that bring temporary happiness. But, until they know they already have permanent access to the light, they may never have true happiness. They may access the light from time to time, but if it cannot be consistent, then neither shall their joy and contentment in this life be sustained.

The true dangers of this life lay waiting for you in the seemingly insignificant, but constant moments of trial and tribulation. The danger lies in the curious child that writes on your wall, and you feel the urge to yell. There is great risk in the moment when your co-worker is rude and you desire to be rude back. There is peril in the instance when you lock yourself out of your house and want to place the blame at someone else's feet. Your happiness can be threatened in the moment you believe that a payment for services rendered is not enough, and you desire to communicate this mistreatment to anyone who will listen.

It is in the outwardly insignificant moments that the power and choice to flip the Gratitude Switch becomes the most crucial. If you can consistently flip the Switch in the small moments of life's difficulties, how much more likely will you be to flip it in life's big moments of despair, hurt, tragedy, and loss?

Before you leave this room, I must give you a final dire warning. If you do not share this with others, you may find yourself forgetting these simple truths and abandoning the use of YOUR Gratitude Switch. This knowledge is much like earthly riches. If you do not properly use this knowledge, it will eventually be lost. But if you put it to work and use it wisely, then it will multiply its net effect on your world and on the world around you.

This will not be an easy task. Life has conditioned you to complain. The Adversary would have you believe that the most comfortable place to reside is in a perpetual state of passing the buck and not being held accountable for your life, your results, your finances, your relationships, your success, and ultimately your own happiness.

Do not give into the common practices of placing blame and engaging in self-victimization. You now understand that the infinite power of gratitude can banish negativity, obliterate the constant feeling of victimhood, and deliver the sweet, blessed state of perpetual bliss.

The key to infinite and unrestrained happiness is the consistent, conscious application of gratitude. If you flip the Gratitude Switch during life's difficult circumstances, no matter how big or how small, you will change your life. By sharing this knowledge, you will change the world. Now go forward and spread the word, my boy. Stand here no more… Take up your banner and go!

With the Eternal Gratitude and Love of a Father,

Patros

Chapter 5

Back to the Real World

After he finished, Jacob stood, and with a reverence usually reserved for a religious text, carefully rolled the note back up and tenderly replaced the string that had bound it.

He took the note and clutched it to his heart. How had he never known these things before? How could he have spent a lifetime seeking joy and fulfillment and never known that the secret to limitless happiness was found in a simple, conscious choice?

Jacob was overwhelmed by the possibility of it all. He had just been delivered his life's mission and the single most valuable thing he could ask for — the key to infinite joy. Patros had told him that success in the task would be marked by his attainment of immeasurable wealth, and somehow, now that he'd received it, that description seemed too simple, too diminutive. This knowledge was so much more.

This knowledge could heal the world.

Jacob knew that he held the answers to so many of life's questions rolled up in his hands and he felt an exhilarating mantle of responsibility come to rest upon his shoulders. He HAD to share this with everyone.

He turned around, forgetting the treasure in the nine counterfeit chests — all of those glittery, earthly materials were so elementary now. He gazed back across the room with only one thought in his mind. He wanted to burst through that door and set about fulfilling his mission with a full awareness of the importance and rewards of doing that very thing.

He delicately removed the key Patros had given him from the red and gold chest and placed it in his pocket before deciding that a pocket didn't seem like the right place to store such an integral item. He wanted it visible, to serve as a reminder of what it had just unlocked.

He took the loop of the small chain that had been holding the key around Patros' neck and ran it through one of his belt loops in the front of his slacks. He wound it through a few more times to shorten the chain, passed the key through one of the chain loops he'd created, and let the key securely dangle in front of his pocket.

He clutched the note in his right hand, firmly enough that there was no risk of it slipping out, but carefully enough that it would not get crumpled or ruined. He began running down the golden tiled path again, but this time, he was using the path to lead him to the rest of his life. He reached the door, flipped the switch off, and shut the door behind him.

It had been raining again. There were puddles littering the sidewalks and potholes on the solitary street. How long had he been in that room? It seemed like hours, or was it minutes?

It felt like dawn was just over the horizon. The night had that quality of the early morning—quiet, but with a noticeable energy in the air. It did not feel like the conclusion of one day; it felt like the beginning of the next.

Jacob stood in front of the red and gold door and remembered the wrinkled, peculiar old man who greeted him there that evening. Where was Patros now? Was he watching Jacob as he said he had done in the past? Feeling Patros' attentive eyes from afar felt comforting, and Jacob was filled with a hope of what would be and what was to come.

He swiveled his head to the right and left. Which way had he come? It didn't matter. What mattered is which way he'd choose to go. That first step in either direction was the first step of the rest of his life. He turned right and began walking with intense strides, hoping to meet someone, anyone with whom he could share this newfound wealth.

Jacob had only taken three steps when… SPLASH!

He stepped right into a deceptively deep and dirty puddle in the sidewalk. His intense step had landed with tremendous force, displacing what seemed like a gallon of water that splashed up nearly three feet. He felt the dirty water seep into his expensive shoes and soak through his socks. He had another sensation of cold water seeping down the entire front of his light-colored slacks.

"No! You've GOT to be kidding me!"

He suddenly felt cold as he stood there, dripping wet, trying to take in what had just happened. He said aloud to no one, "Oh, come on! Did that really JUST happen? After all that I just read and experienced, I ruin the only pair of shoes that I brought on this trip as I'm walking to go help people. And now my pants are stained with the disgusting mud from a disgusting puddle on some ridiculous sidewalk that the city and its ridiculous bureaucracy can't seem to fix. Way to find another way to waste taxpayer dollars!"

As he grunted his last syllable, there was a flash of lightning and a crack of thunder. As if someone has just turned on the shower, it began to pour down rain, all over Jacob, his note, and his enthusiasm for the evening. Jacob couldn't believe his bad luck. The city had hardly received any rainfall all year. Why did it have to decide to come tonight?

He looked around again, desperately seeking shelter. Where WAS he anyway? He wasn't even sure if his hotel was close.

He had a meeting in just a few hours. He pulled out his cell phone to check on the time. It was waterlogged, and the screen was blinking on and off like a fluorescent light flickering its final swan song. He glanced at his watch. This part of the street had no streetlights, making it too dark to read the time.

He suddenly noticed how tired and hungry he was. He paused to take inventory. Totally soaked, completely downtrodden, lost in the city, ruined clothes, damaged phone, tired, hunger pangs, no taxis in site, no idea what direction to walk, going to be late (and wet) to the meeting, and all of it because of Patros, his key, his note, and this street.

Jacob almost squeezed the soggy note in his hand in annoyance as he grumbled loudly and yelled to the sky, as though the clouds were some conduit to the world's concierge desk. "CAN I PLEASE CATCH A BREAK HERE?"

He glanced down at his watch and phone again. Nothing. What could he do? The store windows were dark. The heavy rain had stifled the smell of incense. The street felt empty and hopeless.

Jacob hoped that a car or truck would drive by just so the headlights would shine a light on his sorry situation and illuminate just how bad the damage was.

He just needed some sort of light.

Like an anvil in the head, a thought hit Jacob. The room. The door. The light switch.

Chapter 6

Lessons Learned

He still had Patros' key hanging on his pants, the key that would let him back inside the treasure room. He untwined the key from his belt loop and turned back toward the door. Ah, there it was, in all its beauty. He grabbed the key, inserted it, and turned it with a loud CLICK!

The door swung open, once again revealing the expanse within. He tucked the key into his back pocket in a single movement. There he stood once more in front of the room that had held so much joy and intrigue for him just minutes before. The streetlights had since been turned off so he could not see the start of the golden tiles like he had earlier.

He reached inside and flipped the switch. The room flooded with light for the second time that evening. There, in the center of the room, was his chest and the others. He looked down at the slightly crumpled, wet note in his hand. This note that had been so precious just minutes ago felt like nothing more than a piece of paper as Jacob stood wet, hungry, and cold in the dark. But, now in the light and warmth of the room, he unrolled it again. Luckily, it was all still there. There were a few smears, but all of the text was readable.

His eyes darted back to a passage:

"The key I gave you is a symbol for knowledge. It is something that can be obtained but will be useless if not applied and used in the right way. You knew the red and gold chest contained immeasurable wealth, but you had to choose to use that knowledge as you chose to use the key to unlock it."

Jacob looked down at his wet, dirty pants. There, on the outside of his light-colored slacks, his pocket was wet and dirty — except in one place. There was a completely dry and clean key-shaped spot on his pocket. His startled movements must have pressed the heavy key firmly against his leg, leaving no opportunity for the dirt to reach the part of his pants that was shielded by the key. The surrounding splatter made the outline of the key appear like a small light beige symbol of hope in the midst of the chaotic splatter of filth.

The key. It had unlocked everything.

It had unlocked the room and the chest, and now it had given him the ability to re-enter this room and be reminded of all that he had experienced just moments ago. The key represented knowledge; knowledge that Jacob now chose to use.

He glanced again at the light switch, he flipped it off and on, and again the darkness disappeared and the room was instantly flooded with the light. "The Gratitude Switch," he thought. "How unbelievably simple."

He looked down at his watch that could now be easily seen in the light of the room. It wasn't nearly as late as he thought. He had plenty of time to get back, eat, shower, and get some rest before his big meeting.

Just then, he remembered the card in his left pocket that the cab driver who picked him up from the airport had given him. It was a little soggy, but the phone number was legible. He grabbed his phone, took out the battery, blew it off, and inserted it again. The phone powered up, and he called the number. The driver remembered him, and even remembered his hotel. The driver was also familiar with the neighborhood Jacob had wandered into—and knew exactly where Patros' red and gold door was. He was on his way.

Jacob looked down at the outline of the key again. He gazed at the red and gold chest in the distance. He glanced at the note still in his hand. He fixed his eyes on the light switch that had made it possible for him to see the taxi driver's card and get his phone working again.

That simple flip of the switch really did make all the difference. He read another passage of the note:

"In this room, it was the simple act of flipping the switch that made everything possible. The light allows you to navigate every pitfall, illuminate the path, obtain the key, find the treasure, and significantly improve your chances for success."

"You are now aware that the power of gratitude will illuminate all of life's challenges and allow you to successfully navigate anything that may come your way, but that light will be unavailable to you if you don't make the mindful, daily decision to flip your Gratitude Switch in order to access the light. Think of the flipping of the switch as the simple act of choosing to consciously express, feel, and experience gratitude no matter what life may throw at you."

Jacob exhaled slowly, as if blowing out the air of frustration that took up residence inside him after he stepped in the puddle. In that moment, he consciously chose to flip the Gratitude Switch and find everything in his immediate situation he could be thankful for.

He looked down at his pants. "I'm so lucky that I brought other clothes with me for my meeting!"

He looked at his phone. "I'm really glad they make phones durable enough to withstand a little water. Besides, even if it hadn't worked, I can go to a store tomorrow and get another one. What an incredible world of technology and convenience we live in."

He glanced down at his shoes. "I sure am glad I listened to that salesperson and invested in good footwear. These shoes look like they are perfectly fine. They just need to dry a little."

He looked at the taxi driver's card. "I am grateful that this driver gave me his card. What a lesson in marketing. In fact, that reminds me, I need to re-order business cards. Maybe I can put one of Patros' quotes on there so everyone who has a card can read a few words of the wisdom that I learned here tonight."

He took a deep breath. "I'm alive, what a blessing! What a night! What a lesson!"

He then gazed at the ceiling, as if trying to carry his voice past its beams and shingles so that it may find Patros, wherever he may be. "I get it Patros, I understand. I just have to flip the switch, and all will be well!"

He felt a rush of gratitude for Patros, for the evening, for this room, and for life! He felt those lingering wisps of frustration melt away, and now it was Jacob whose smile wrinkles seemed to deepen, just as the taxi pulled up outside.

Jacob peered down at the last lines in the note:

"By sharing this knowledge, you will change the world. Now go forward and spread the word, my boy. Stand here no more… Take up your banner and go!"

Jacob went, knowing exactly what he was going to talk to the taxi driver about on the way back to the hotel.

PART II

FLIPping
Foundations

Chapter 1

A Tale of Two Men

This is a story of two men living similar, yet different lives. In this brief tale, you will see the problem we as the human family are currently facing, and you will begin to gain insight to the simple tool that will change your world and the world around you. The story may be about two men, but you will probably see yourself in both of these individuals — and whether you are a man or a woman, one of their stories may likely be YOUR story.

**It was the best of times for one man.
It was the worst of times for another.**

Two alarms go off on a Monday morning at 6:30 a.m. Man #1 opens his eyes to greet the day in his gorgeous five-bedroom home, the perfect size for his growing children and beautiful wife. As *Man #2* hears the alarm, he opens his eyes to glare at the water stain on the ceiling above his head as he mumbles about how his aging, three-bedroom house is only good for draining his bank account.

Rubbing the sleep from his eyes, *Man #1* lays still for a moment and feels his heart beating, takes a deep breath, and marvels at how great he feels after a good night's rest. *Man #2* runs his hands down to his belly and all of its excess pounds that he wishes would somehow magically fall off (because who has time to work out).

Both men know it's time to get up. Man #1 takes another deep breath and feels a rush of excitement about the start of a new day that is full of untold potential. Sometimes it's hard to separate his dreams from reality since he has his *dream* job, lives in his *dream* home, and is married to his *dream* wife.

Man #2 takes another deep breath (more like a sigh) and feels the sting of regret from staying up too late watching reality TV. "Great," he thinks, "*now I'll be useless all day.*" He pauses, dreading to put his feet on the ground and spend another day working at a thankless job, going nowhere, being underpaid, and despising his boss. If *only* he had time to find a better job.

Man #1 swings his legs out of bed as two words of prayer quietly cross his lips so as to not wake his wife. *"Thank you!"* He glances over at the love of his life and feels a rush of gratefulness for how she selflessly stays at home to care for the children. He's thankful he hasn't woken her; she deserves the extra rest since her job is exponentially harder than his.

Man #2 reluctantly swings his legs out of bed, saying aloud, "Geez I'm tired," hoping to make as much noise as possible to remind his wife that he is the one who has to go to work while she gets to stay home and *only* take care of the kids. He hopes she realizes how lucky she is that she doesn't have to go out and get a *real* job. He looks at her with a mixture of envy and resentment and thinks, *"Oh no, please don't get up. I'm sure you need all the rest you can get!"*

Both men leave their bedrooms and head down the hall. *Man #1* does some jumping jacks, pushups, and crunches before sitting down at the kitchen table to study the Scriptures. He reads, carefully looking for the lesson he knows he will inevitably learn from his studies. He kneels, utters a prayer of gratitude, and pleads for a productive and powerful day. He relishes the opportunity to connect with God daily.

Man #2 slumps to his knees with his hands clasped together and goes through the motions of prayer. He knows he's supposed to be religious, so he utters an all too common series of robotic phrases, hurriedly trying to complete the ritual so he can check it off his list.

After his satisfying prayer, *Man #1* takes ten minutes to meditate and clear his mind. He then pulls out a book on personal development and begins reading. He loves to fill his head with thoughts of success in the morning. He looks at his vision board and feels the fulfillment of achieving so many of the items. He reads the affirmations he's written and writes down a few words in his journal.

After his empty prayer, *Man #2* plops down on the couch and reaches for the remote. He is already fed up with the day and thinks that ten minutes of sports highlights might put him in a better mood. Then he thinks, *"A few more minutes of shut eye can't hurt. I was up late; I deserve it."* He falls back asleep. A ten-minute nap turns into a thirty-minute snooze. He abruptly awakens and feels stress wash over him. *"Oh great, now I'm gonna be late."*

Both men make their way to the bathroom and turn on the shower. *Man #1* hops in and feels a rush of excitement as the warm water splashes over his head. He knows that some of his most inspired ideas come to him in the shower. He bends down and picks up a few of the kids' toys off the bathtub floor. As he puts them away, he smiles at the thought of those gorgeous, funny kids and the bath games he played with them the night before.

Man #2 steps into the lukewarm shower, grumbling about the "stupid water heater" needing to be replaced. He plops down on the bathtub floor and feels the acute pain of a bath toy digging into his backside. "Why can't the kids clean up after themselves?" he mutters as he tries to enjoy the water that is now too hot. He sits there feeling a sense of dread that in less than one hour, he will be sitting in an uncomfortable chair, pounding a keyboard, and doing pointless work.

Both men make their way to their closets. Man #1 gazes at his many fine suits, beautiful shirts, and collection of silk ties. He looks at the tie from last Sunday and smiles. He had used the corner of his tie to wipe away a few pieces of mushy baby snack from his baby boy's face. The tie almost seems more beautiful because of it. He picks a dark suit, a tailored French cuff shirt, and a tie that compliments both. He selects a silk pocket square, slides on his expensive shoes, and takes a glance in the mirror as he thinks, *"Not too bad!"* He's not required to wear a suit, but he loves the way it feels—and a little extra effort can't hurt anything.

Man #2 looks at his limited suit selection, his shirts that feel too familiar and old, and his ties, a few of which are slightly stained. He pushes those ties aside as he wonders why his wife insists on feeding the baby such messy food. He decides he is not going to wear a suit that day. *"Who am I trying to impress?"* He grabs a pair of khakis that seem a little tight and pulls a polo shirt over his head that seems to showcase a little too much of his growing belly. *"If I have to go to a crappy job, I deserve to be comfortable!"*

Both men head to the kitchen. Knowing his family will be up soon, Man #1 prepares breakfast for them. He fixes a warm batch of oatmeal and leaves it on the stove for his kids. He sits down to enjoy his hot bowl of oats as he listens to a book on success principles. Man #2 grabs a bowl of sugary cereal, trying to chew as quietly as possible so he doesn't wake up the kids and get forced into making their breakfast.

Just as both men finish their breakfasts, the kids and wives come into the kitchen. Man #1 greets his family and showers them with love, hugs, and kisses. He dishes up their oatmeal as he makes small talk about what they dreamed about and how they slept. He helps his wife by tidying up the kitchen and squeezes out a few extra minutes with his family before he leaves; hoping that the small things he did will make the day a little easier for his wife.

Man #2 also greets his family with an obligatory, yet enjoyable batch of hugs and kisses, but is immediately taken back by how loud the kids are talking. He tries to quiet them as he reluctantly gets bowls and pours cereal for them, hoping to move quickly, so he can get out the door to his uncomfortable but quiet office. He tries to find an excuse why he must leave right away.

Both men grab their laptops, kiss their families goodbye, and walk to their cars. Man #1 opens the door of his sporty sedan and fires up the engine. He pauses to reflect on the blessing of having a comfortable, working vehicle. He looks at the gas gauge—it's almost on empty—but he has plenty to get to work. He presses play on his latest audio book on success to take advantage of the drive time. He pulls up his bank account balance on his phone and feels an overwhelming gratitude for the incredible abundance that he and his family enjoy. He backs out of the driveway to go create even more abundance by providing value and serving others. He feels an exhilarating optimism and knows that although life may throw a curve ball at him today, he is perfectly equipped to take on any challenge.

Man #2 opens the door to his sedan and is reminded that it isn't the car he wanted. He looks at the gas gauge and feels distraught that the gas is so low. He hopes there's enough gas to get to work and then wonders if he can even afford to buy gas before his next payday. His bank account balance reveals that he has enough for gas, and that's about it—just another reminder of his pointless job where he works for pennies. He pulls out of the driveway wondering how little he can get away with doing at the office. He wonders what will go wrong during the day, because something always does.

****

These two men have many similarities, and yet, what different lives they lead. Both men are married with children and are homeowners. Both wake up in the morning to prepare for a workday and go through their respective morning routines. Both say goodbye to their families, get into their vehicles, and drive to work.

That is about where the similarities end.
The differences, however, abound.

One man has a beautiful home, while the other has a home in need of desperate repair. One man has a fit body, while Man #2 is overweight and unhappy about that fact, but is unwilling to take action to change it. Man #1 is living his dream life. Man #2 despises his job and, seemingly, his life. He echoes the feelings of a large percentage of today's workforce who feel underpaid and underappreciated.

Man #1 views his wife's role in the home quite differently than Man #2 does, and he also seems to have a sharply different opinion of his children. Man #1 is disciplined and interested in doing what is required to be successful. Man #2 is interested in doing what he must to survive. Both men seem to think that prayer is important, but for very different reasons. For Man #1, the shower is an opportunity. For Man #2, it's a nuisance. They even feel differently when it comes to their children using their ties as wearable napkins.

Man #1 chooses a healthy breakfast and a healthy attitude about fixing food for his family; Man #2 wants to shovel sugary cereal into his face and get the heck outta Dodge. When Man #1 looks at his bank account, he feels security and abundance. Man #2 suffers under the weight of lack and want, but he's seems unwilling to change his fate.

Man #1 is clearly an optimist who believes life really is a glass half full, and in many cases, overflowing.

Man #2 is a pessimist and a skeptic (he'd probably call himself a "realist") who thinks that life is one cruel, glass-half-empty joke.

Who are these two men who seem to live such different lives?

They are both... ME.

I have been both of these men at different points in my life. Unfortunately, Man #2's thoughts and actions are the ones I most closely mirrored... **that is, before I discovered the eternal and life altering power of gratitude.**

The conversion from being ungrateful to being someone who lives with the constant companion of gratitude has been a lengthy and difficult one. I wish I'd had a mentor who helped me through the process, some gentle soul who would have left breadcrumbs for me along the way. There was no gentle soul or wise mentor. Life itself — with its hardships and trials — was my cold and relentless teacher.

Nonetheless, I am left to wonder, what if I could have had someone to guide me through the journey toward becoming Man #1? What I'm sharing with you in this book is what I wish someone would have shared with me. I'm not going to simply give you platitudes like "be more thankful" or "just have an attitude of gratitude." I'm not going to give you overused suggestions that frankly rarely work for most people, or say things like, "keep a gratitude journal" and "just go on a gratitude walk." I'm going to give you substance. I'm going to share with you real information and a real formula that will virtually guarantee your success.

How did I come to realize the importance of gratitude and learn how to make it an actionable game changer in my life? Read on, my friends. The next chapter will enlighten you.

Chapter 2

From Out of the Depths

There was a time in my life when I knew I'd hit rock bottom.

You know when you've reached it because "rock bottom" is that unmistakable moment when you find the power and the strength you've been lacking to change your today and go on to create a better tomorrow.

To better explain my rock bottom, we need to back up a few years from that moment and discover together where it all went so horribly wrong.

Searching for Something Outside the Walls

In 2007, I sat in a gray walled cubicle in Salt Lake City, and that's how I felt.

Just... Gray.

After ending my sparkling and rewarding career as a glorified telemarketing associate where I had worked for a large mortgage and auto finance company, I was now working as an independent mortgage broker. It wasn't the most exciting job in the world, but I needed it to pay the bills and support my soon-to-be wife and the family we were thinking of starting. I was still a glorified telemarketing associate, but now I had a license that allowed me to take those phone calls I was making and turn them into real cash with mortgage refinances.

This one particular day, as I sat in my ergonomically correct chair, staring at the gray walls of my cubicle, I decided to take a departure from the stale phone leads I had sitting on my desk and get busy by hustling up some fresh mortgage leads. I called a good friend who was active in the real estate business and told him if he needed help facilitating any of his loans; I might be able to provide some answers.

He politely declined—but he got back in touch with me a short time later about another matter entirely.

He and another good friend of mine were considering starting a business together, and they were having a meeting later that week to discuss it. They asked if I would be interested in meeting with them to consider a new business venture.

Any future that didn't involve cubed, monochrome walls sounded good to me—and so I decided to go.

I instantly caught a vision of something that had the potential to be so massive that there was no way I *wasn't* going to get involved—and it was literally a matter of days before the three of us were in business together. We soon opened the doors of REIC, which stood for Real Estate Investors Club. After a few years, we rebranded ourselves as Strongbrook before expanding our company nationally.

If you have ever been involved in a new business, you know that it takes a constant application of the principles of success and abundance in order to actually see the business succeed past the growing pains.

And that's where I ran into my first big problem.

I was an entitled brat who was filled with excuses and negativity, and worst of all, I didn't even know it. Victimhood and a lack of personal accountability were the prevailing factors guiding my mindset as I entered this ownership agreement with my friends.

The way I interacted with life was a far cry from actual reality, but because I had never been taught a different way of thinking, the negativity I chose to see was the only reality I knew.

A virus has a way of making everything around it sick, and this virus of the mind that I was afflicted with had taken up a permanent home in my brain. But because I was completely oblivious to it, I did nothing to destroy or even treat the virus during those pivotal years of our company's founding.

After a few painful and telling experiences when it became crystal clear that my business partners and some of our clients had been hurt by my attitude and actions—or better said, *lack* of action—I realized that I needed to make some changes.

If you want to hear the compelling story of one of those pivotal moments in the early days of our company's founding, visit kevinclayson.com and click on the "Entrepreneur On Fire Podcast" link and go to episode 521.

Eradicating the Virus

By 2009, I had embarked upon a much-needed personal development journey. I began reading and listening to countless books and programs, and I invested money I didn't have into seminars, mentors, and online courses, because I knew that unless I invested both time and money into myself, I would never become the success I'd always hoped to become.

Those dollars and that time were the most valuable investments I've ever made.

One of the most life changing events I attended was "The Big Money Speaker Bootcamp" in the summer of 2010. This event was put on by a man I would later hire to be my personal coach and mentor, ABC's *Secret Millionaire*, two-time College Speaker of the Year, and co-author of *Chicken Soup for the College Soul*, James Malinchak.

Thanks to James, his content, and his straightforward approach to the speaking business and the business of being an author, I started to believe that I too could train and speak and that maybe I could even write a book one day.

With my newfound knowledge and increased self-belief, I asked my partners if they would take a risk and let me do some speaking and training for our company. They agreed—and you won't believe what happened.

I was actually pretty good at it.

My messages resonated with audiences, and I found myself using my newfound skill set to train and teach our employees as well, and we saw our company culture shift and overall employee contentment and production increase. At that time, our company had grown to over fifty employees, and I was starting to become known as the go-to voice of inspiration, beacon of hope, and a source of (gasp) wisdom inside of the walls of our company.

I quickly became Strongbrook's most requested speaker nationwide and was soon jet setting from coast to coast to give keynote presentations, deliver workshops, and make cameo appearances as an owner and co-founder of a revolutionary company. I even created a few talks that I was occasionally asked to give to other growing companies in the area.

There I was, speaking, inspiring, and getting compensated to give talks. I was starting to feel more confident in my abilities and knowledge. I also felt I was making more personal progress, and I was certainly experiencing more success than ever before.

Riding that high lasted for about a year; that is, until we made a single hiring decision that changed my life. The man we hired—let's call him Frank—became our new Marketing Director.

Little did I know that I would allow this one hiring decision to derail everything I had started to accomplish.

The Downward Spiral

Frank was a guy who knew his stuff. He had already experienced some massive success at a young age, and when we brought him on, he quickly put us on the path to starting a new company inside our existing Strongbrook umbrella.

In 2010, we created a direct sales side of our company called Strongbrook Direct. This new enterprise—and what would eventually become thousands of independent reps—was tasked to market and promote our real estate products across the country using a multi-level, network marketing-type framework.

Frank was instrumental in helping us set up, establish, and oversee this new direct sales and network marketing arm, and for that reason, we moved him into the position of Managing Director of Strongbrook Direct.

Although my partners and I were involved in the running of all areas of our business, Frank ultimately had autonomy inside this new division. And in the beginning, he was utilizing me as the primary trainer and speaker. I'd travel across the country to speak to our growing team of independent sales reps.

At first, all the traveling and speaking felt exhilarating. I was excited to work alongside Frank and my fellow founders to make this division the most profitable arm our company had ever seen.

But my excitement was short-lived.

A few months after he started working with us, Frank and I began to butt heads. We never seemed to see eye-to-eye on ANYTHING. There was an uncomfortable and palpable tension between us, and it exploded into full-volume shouting matches on a number of occasions.

The tension and dislike between us transcended business and became personal. At one point, Frank shouted at me that he was offended by the love I expressed for my wife on social media. His words were, "It's really sad that your relationship with your wife is so bad that you can't even tell her you love her in person."

Things got even nastier, and I chose to become angry and hurt, especially after what felt like a series of personal attacks. I got loud, he got loud and pretty soon we could scarcely stand to be in the same room together.

As a result of our increasing differences, Frank felt like he could not trust me to be a valid contributor of any kind. In Frank's defense, I had proven time and time again that I had not dealt with my deep seated sense of entitlement and victim's mentality. Even after finding success in our business, I had yet to purge these attitudes from my life, and consequently, they would surface at inopportune times.

I became an active participant in the destruction of our relationship. I would pretend I respected Frank in public, but in private, I berated and criticized him to anyone who would listen.

By the end of 2011, I was utterly miserable. It was a gradual shift that took place over the course of many months, but as I reflect back, it feels as though it all turned on a dime. I went from feeling needed and successful to feeling unappreciated and marginalized.

Perhaps even worse, it was as if all of that personal development I'd experienced had never even taken place.

I was once again full of complaints and had reverted back to my role as the poor, persecuted victim. I was no longer acting like an owner or a founder of the company. I again adopted an *employee mindset* — I showed up, did as little as possible, and expected a paycheck.

If I was not speaking and traveling, I found myself bitter, resentful, discontent, and somehow I had devolved back to the man from four years earlier who did not want to do much work, but who had this insatiable desire to be recognized for what he perceived as his many contributions.

Through a combination of fatigue from constant travel and the proliferated exhaustion I felt due to the fact that our baby boy Braxton did not understand the concept of sleeping through the night at the time, I had become unbelievably depressed, fatigued, and unsatisfied.

I was on my way to the bottom.

Each morning, I'd wake up feeling exhausted and resentful. I didn't want to get out of bed and face my thankless job or Frank. I would spend many mornings sitting on the shower floor wondering how I was supposed to get through the day.

I had no desire to engage in personal development or success training of any kind, and I spent every free moment mindlessly watching Netflix, sports, or reality TV. If I wasn't engaging in soul-numbing entertainment, I was on social media pretending life was peachy.

I was a mildly attentive father, but I relished my alone time. I was a difficult man to live with—so quick to become angry at insignificant things because of the self-imposed stress I was experiencing.

My colleagues all became "idiots" for not seeing my potential.

My car wasn't good enough.

My house wasn't good enough.

No matter how much money was in the account, I would stare at the balance and feel a tremendous amount of scarcity.

Sound familiar? Yes, this is the point in my life when I became Man #2 from "A Tale of Two Men."

Welcome to Rock Bottom

One day, after another routinely dreadful morning, I sat in my car looking at our office and thinking, "I DO NOT want to go in there. I hate my job. I can't stand Frank. I don't make enough money. I am so underutilized! Should I leave the company? Would I even be missed? What's the point of all this anyway? Is this *really* my life? This can't be my life."

And there it was. I had finally reached it—I was at rock bottom.

As I mentioned, I believe rock bottom is the moment when you finally find the power and the strength you've always been lacking to change your today and go on to create a better tomorrow.

I knew I couldn't get any lower, and at that moment, I realized that all of the training, coaching, reading, and inspiring I'd engaged in just a few years earlier had not disappeared completely.

I started to sense something deep within.

There was still a tiny spark of hope that things could get better.

That internal spark was like a smothered flame that just needed a little air, and as soon as I realized the spark was there, it was as if someone poured kerosene on it. I started to think:

"If my circumstances won't change, maybe I can change the way I look at my circumstances, and maybe as a result, they actually WILL change."

It seemed half crazy, and part of me doubted it would work. But almost as soon as I *flipped that internal switch* and began questioning the way I was looking at things, some of the powerful coaching I'd received came flooding into my mind.

During the Big Money Speaker Bootcamp I attended in 2010, I heard a man speak named Darren Hardy. Darren is a success mentor to CEO's and high performance achievers, as well as an accomplished speaker and best-selling author. (darrenhardy.com)

That talk would end up changing my life… two years after I heard it.

Darren had discussed how small daily actions could compound into big results. He planted the seed that day, and I scrambled around to find the notes I had taken during his talk. On the page, I had written, *"Pick a frustration I have and keep a gratitude journal about that thing for twenty one days."*

The word "gratitude" jumped off the page at me and caused me to rethink everything I was currently going through.

I recalled Darren's story about how he kept a gratitude journal for his wife and then gave it to her after a year of compiling entries. It sounded like a great idea at the time, and I had decided to try it.

Sadly, I never stuck with it.

But now, two years later, maybe this was the time to start again. I thought if I started writing something down every day in a journal, maybe such an act would be enough to change the way I viewed my circumstances.

Why Gratitude Journaling Didn't Work For Me

Not long after I had decided to start a journal for the second time, fear flooded my consciousness, and I felt that little flame almost go out. I thought, "This can't be the answer. The act of journaling and trying to feel gratitude for the things in my life had not worked once before, so why would it work now?"

The overused Einstein quote came to mind. You know, it's the one that defines *insanity* as "doing the same thing but expecting a different result."

I already felt bad enough; I didn't want to add insanity to the mix.

Even so, there was still something inside me that told me not to dismiss this whole *gratitude* thing just yet. That's when I decided to diagnose why the journal didn't work for me. If I could figure out where things broke down, maybe I could create a new path around the breakdown and move forward.

After I heard Darren Hardy speak two years before, I had purchased two gratitude journals—one for my wife, and one for my daughter. I faithfully wrote in those journals for about two weeks, recounting what I loved and appreciated about the two girls in my life.

At the time, I didn't realize my mistake.

Upon reflection, I came to realize that I was just writing about things that were *already* good. As a result, it didn't produce any kind of massive internal shift, so I didn't stick with it. In fact, I let the practice go dormant long before it became a habit.

The idea of gratitude still held no real power for me. At the time, it was nothing more than "feeling sort of thankful for good stuff every now and then." I still did not understand THE ONE singular truth about gratitude that would make the difference.

During my first gratitude journaling attempt, I was simply hoping to *feel* a little more thankful. I was operating under the mistaken idea that gratitude was just some emotional "thingy."

And that wasn't going to cut it.

My Gratitude Breakthrough

Passively journaling about something that already made me feel good was not going to be enough. I was at rock bottom, and I was not interested in staying there, so I chose to try something different. I made a recurring task in my iPhone to remind me every morning at 8am to "Feel Gratitude Today."

Nice idea, right?

There was a problem.

The reminder would pop up on my task list for each day. I don't know how YOU interact with YOUR to-do lists, but I am really skilled at procrastinating when it comes to mine. What I had effectively done was turn feeling gratitude *into a job.*

Even though my new approach wasn't perfect, it seemed to be working better than the gratitude journal. I was choosing to seek gratitude more often, but there were still days when I just "couldn't get around" to feeling any gratitude at all.

I decided to change up my strategy a little and try something a little different. Next, I tried finding something to be thankful for the moment my alarm buzzed. I would look around the instant my reminder sounded and search for something to be thankful for in that moment. Maybe it was my wife; maybe it was my kids; maybe it was that I woke up at all. It didn't matter—I just tried to find something.

I started making more progress, but I was not satisfied with the velocity of my personal and emotional recovery from rock bottom. I still wasn't activating gratitude; rather, I was casually waiting for some moment when I could *feel* gratitude.

I decided to go back to my notes from Darren Hardy's talk and see if there was any additional information that could give me some much needed guidance.

It was then that I discovered the secret.

I once again saw that line that had sparked this whole gratitude experiment in the first place. THIS time, when I read the sentence, a different word popped off the page.

> *"Pick a **frustration** I have and keep a gratitude journal about that thing for twenty one days."*

I instantly fixated on the word "frustration." Maybe that was the key. I decided to look for a frustration, and whenever it showed up, I would consciously feel gratitude in that moment for THAT frustration, or at least attempt to find gratitude IN that frustration.

Cracking the Code

I began to pick one frustrating or difficult experience, take a moment, reflect on it, and then find a way to feel gratitude for something embedded within that frustration—or at least try to become thankful for what I learned from the experience.

Here are a few examples:

- One day, a flying rock chipped the windshield of my new car and subsequently caused a big crack. I thought, "At least the whole windshield didn't shatter and I'm still safe."
- My baby wrote with crayon on our white walls, and I thought, "It's okay. I'm just thankful the little guy is healthy and curious. Besides, I will look at the crayon on this wall one day and WISH he were still this age."
- I woke up in the morning and stubbed my toe on the bed, and I decided to be thankful I had a bed at all. "I didn't have to sleep on the floor last night, and I have a roof over my head."
- A car cut me off, and I squashed my road rage. "I'm so thankful he didn't clip me and we avoided an accident. Plus, who knows what he or she is personally going through. It's no big deal because I'm safe, and I hope this person gets to his/her destination safely."
- Frank made a snide remark at work, and I thought, "I'm really thankful he's here, because it means I don't have to do his job AND mine, and I can focus on something that brings me more joy."

Each time, after discovering and acknowledging a frustration, I located something I could feel grateful for embedded within the frustration. Then I would choose to pause for a moment and actually *experience* gratitude for it.

Life began to transform before my eyes. No longer was I taking one little frustration and milking it all day so I could go home and seek sympathy from my wife and kids by saying, "Wow, look at how rough I had it today. Pity me."

I had finally stopped focusing on the tiny frustrations that are so common, which meant that each step got a little lighter and each day felt a little more hopeful. I was starting to experience what my friend Hal Elrod calls "soulful gratitude," which is the kind of gratitude where you feel real, palpable emotion move inside you.

I began to see that if I didn't let the little frustrations alter my mood and the course of the day, I was far more likely to take the bigger problems and life-altering events in stride—and maybe even find gratitude for the big stuff.

And a Verb Is Born

So that was it—the *big secret* that was hiding under my nose the entire time. Let's review the ONE step that was missing from my previous attempts to feel more grateful…

On second thought, I need to make something perfectly clear before we continue. If you don't understand this idea, this entire book will be pointless. So, stand up and do a few jumping jacks. Wake up and get ready because you have got to get this.

Are you ready? Drumroll please...

YOU CAN MAKE GRATITUDE AN ACTIVE, DAILY OCCUR-
RENCE... NOT BY BEING GRATEFUL FOR THE STUFF THAT'S AL-
READY GOOD, BUT BY FINDING THE "GOOD" EMBEDDED WITHIN
THE "BAD" AND BECOMING THANKFUL FOR THAT.

Once I realized this truth, it became my guiding process to create more happiness, contentment, control, and success. I started to feel gratitude fueling my life.

It was by going through an internal process of finding a frustration and activating gratitude for the frustration that I began to call it "flipping the gratitude switch" — and that is how the FLIP Formula was born.

I had stumbled upon a secret switch that we all have, a switch that can immediately illuminate all of life's challenges and shine light in the dark places of your life — and that's when it dawned on me:

If I can FLIP a single moment, it could change the trajectory of my day...

If I can FLIP enough days, it could change the trajectory of my week...

If I can FLIP enough weeks, it could change the trajectory of my month...

Months turn into years, and years turn into a lifetime...

I had cracked the code to never having a bad day again.

Once I discovered the power of gratitude, I began searching for the definitive guidebook or some sort of how-to manual on thankfulness, but I was unable to find the right guide to help me navigate the process.

There are about a billion (or so) gratitude journals on Amazon, lots of books on the scientific and positive effects of gratitude, and about a million more books that mention how gratitude is a big key to success, happiness, and wealth, but I still couldn't find what I really needed.

The "secret sauce" that I had discovered seemed to be missing from everyone else's happiness recipes. I had been searching for, but unable to locate, the most important truth about tapping into the eternal and unlimited power of gratitude...

GRATITUDE IS AN ACTION, NOT AN EMOTION. GRATITUDE IS
SOMETHING YOU DO, NOT JUST SOMETHING YOU FEEL!

Through this whole learning process, gratitude became something I actively started doing daily, regularly, even hourly, and *THAT* is what caused life to *REALLY* change for me. I finally abandoned the thought that gratitude was a noun, and I embraced the fact that gratitude was an active, powerful, and exciting *VERB*.

Chapter 3

There's a New Verb in Town

Doing vs. Feeling
I want to make sure you understand the key idea that gratitude is a verb and not the traditional, Webster-dumbed-down version of it being a "thing." We need to eradicate this ludicrous idea that gratitude is just some little thing you feel. We need to stop thinking of gratitude as a touchy feely emotion that washes over us from time to time. We also need to stop thinking that gratitude is just a sensation we get when things go well.

Gratitude is something you DO, not just something you *feel*.

You deserve to experience all the happiness, fulfillment, joy, and control you want in life; the rest of this book will help you do exactly that if you let it. There is, however, some critical information that you must possess if you are ever to truly wrap your mind and heart around what gratitude really is. One of my favorite quotes on gratitude, is given by a man I highly respect named Dieter F. Uchtdorf. He says:

> *"It is easy to be grateful for things when life seems to be going our way. But what then of those times when what we wish for seems to be far out of reach?*
> *Could I suggest that we see gratitude as a disposition, a way of life that stands independent of our current situation? In other words, I'm suggesting that instead of being thankful for things, we focus on being thankful in our circumstances – whatever they may be."*

I love this idea of being thankful **IN** our current circumstances whatever they may be, because it indicates that gratitude is something we must **DO** during life's frustrations, not just something we **FEEL** when everything is going well.
Gratitude, therefore, is not a noun or an emotion like many people think it is. Gratitude is something we can control, something we can activate, and something we can trigger. In short, gratitude is a VERB! I discovered that the secret to using gratitude to change my life was to view it as an *action*.

Let the Verbification Begin

In order to make gratitude an active participant in my life, it needed to become like doing a push-up or a sit-up. Gratitude needed to become something that may be hard to do in the moment, but by choosing to exercise it anyway, it could strengthen me.

The process was not easy at first, but with a constant and consistent exercising of my gratitude muscles, the weight of life's trials and tribulations became much easier to bear.

Part of the reason most people haven't been able to see gratitude for the true key to happiness that it can be is because we've been taught that gratitude is a noun — more specifically, a thing.

A *thing* is something we casually refer to and perhaps use from time to time. For most people, gratitude has been a thing like a trashcan or like gum on the bottom of our shoe. It's this *thing* or *feeling* that exists; that we interact with as the occasion calls for it.

The problem with "things" is that we pay attention to them only when they are relevant to us in specific moments. This makes such things easy to forget after we use them.

Gratitude is **not** a thing like a boy band or celebrity gossip.

Gratitude is **not** a thing like the latest viral funny cat video.

Gratitude is **not** a thing that goes out of style over time like a pair of bell-bottoms, a Molly Ringwald movie, or a Sony Walkman.

Gratitude is **not** some personal development fad or mystical "Secret" that will sweep the nation for a brief period before it fades into the background.

Gratitude will never go out of style.

It's important for gratitude to become a sustainable movement, not a fad. It needs to become an all-consuming swell in our collective consciousness. And most importantly, if gratitude is going to become a movement, it has to contain *action.*

Movement implies action…

Actions are described by verbs…

And that, my friends, is why Gratitude is a VERB.

The way to access the unlimited and unrestrained power of gratitude in your life is by making it an actionable event. To help explain this, I am now going to make up a word:

Verbify: *The act of turning a noun into a verb by applying a massive amount of conscious effort and thought to the aforementioned noun, with the specific purpose of changing the very nature of how you interact and understand said noun.* (#websterskillz)

We need to verbify gratitude!

Shedding Pounds of Discontentment

When I started to enact gratitude in this way — when I *verbified* it in

56

my life—and acknowledged that its real power was found by initiating it and making it actionable, it was kind of like intensifying a workout routine in order to lose weight more quickly.

Maybe you've tried to lose weight before and thought, "If I walk a little more every day, I could accelerate my results." After all, there is no doubt you will burn more calories if you exercise for longer periods of time.

But, what if you started *jogging* for the same amount of time that you had spent walking? If I were to walk for 30 minutes at a 2.0 mph pace, I would burn a little over 100 calories. However, if I were to run for 30 minutes at a 6.0 mph pace, I would burn around 400 calories.

Walking and running are similar actions, require the same equipment (your body and some shoes), and can each be performed for exactly the same amount of time—but are you going to lose weight more quickly by walking for half an hour or running for the same amount of time?

Running will shed the weight faster, right?

If you are carrying around ten, 25, or even 100 pounds of discontentment and "why me" attitudes about life, then consider the FLIP Formula to be the fastest and most effective way to shed all that unwanted *mind fat*.

Consider this marathon training for your brain.

What the FLIP?

FLIPping the Gratitude Switch is a description of what I believe we can do—on the inside—to change the trajectory of any given moment and deliver unrestrained joy and control in our lives. FLIPping the Gratitude Switch **IS** the "verbification" that gratitude needs in order to become the game changer for you that it has become for me.

When I refer to "FLIPping the Gratitude Switch," you'll notice that I capitalize the first half of the letters in the word FLIPping. This is because F.L.I.P. is an acronym that represents the four steps of the FLIP Formula.

FLIPping the Gratitude Switch is a process that I was using long before I turned the idea into a teachable formula. In the beginning, I knew I had stumbled upon some sort of "happiness life hack," but I wasn't sure how I could explain what was happening. I just knew I was turning on or flipping what felt like a switch inside of me when life handed me frustrations.

Thanks to coaches, family, and friends, I found a way to create and articulate the formula with the help of the phrase I'd been using all along to describe what I had been feeling.

Buckle up for an exhilarating journey of AWESOME, and let's get to FLIPpin.'

Chapter 4

Let's Get to FLIPpin'

According to a recent Harris Poll, one-third of us are, well, kind of miserable.

The study was conducted using a series of questions to determine Americans' levels of contentment and life satisfaction. The study found 33% of those polled did not consider themselves to be "very happy."

They cited potential causes such as deteriorating economic conditions, rising college tuition costs, mounting debt, and increasing levels of underemployment and unemployment. Regardless of what was causing the lack of happiness, I was shocked that so few people found happiness in their current situations.

Did you ever read *Winnie the Pooh* stories or watch the cartoons as a child? If you have kids of your own, you probably read *Winnie the Pooh* stories to them or watched Pooh together. And, if you are familiar with that honey loving bear, then you probably also know Eeyore.

Eeyore is one sad donkey. He sees things from a "glass is totally empty" perspective. He also suffers from the complete inability to experience pleasure from activities most other people find enjoyable. Even his home in the Hundred Acre Woods is officially named "Eeyore's Gloomy Place: Rather Boggy and Sad."

From where I sit, it seems that we are a nation, and really a human family, full of way too many Eeyores. We have a tendency to expect the worst, think negatively, and constantly speak words of pessimism into our lives.

I say it's time to shift our collective focus and stop being sad, old gray asses (err, donkeys). I think Alfred D. Souza summed it up best when he said:

> "For a long time, it seemed to me that life was about to begin — real life. But there was always some obstacle in the way, something to be gotten through first, some unfinished business, time to still be served, a debt to be paid. Then life would begin.
> "At last it dawned on me that these obstacles <u>were</u> my life.
> "This perspective has helped me to see that there is no way to happiness.
> "Happiness is the way."

Life *is* challenging. At times there seems to be a nonstop barrage of challenges. And, now that we've gotten that inconvenient truth out of the way, we can move past it and start finding the joy in life. And, not just in the life you think you want... but in the life you are living right now!

A Modern Epidemic

Whether or not you would have answered "unhappy" in the Harris Poll, you could stand to be little happier, right? Who would say no to a little more joy in their life? After all, we spend our lives chasing what we are sure will make us happy.

And yet, so few of us seem to find it.

Whether it is at work, in school, or in our relationships, we are always searching for the latest, greatest thing that will bring us satisfaction and contentment. In fact, we are so busy trying to find ways to be happy that we don't have time to ever learn how to *actually be* happy.

Many of you don't know it, but right now, right where you sit, you have been afflicted with a deadly disease.

It's called watitingforthefutureitis.

We spend a lifetime thinking the next job will be the one that will finally let us get ahead. We spend a lifetime thinking, "If I can just get that promotion, everything will finally be better." We think we have to increase our income before we can live a life of freedom. We think that the next car will be the one we want, and the next house will be our dream house.

We don't realize that, with a little applied effort, happiness can be found...

Right. This. Moment.

In fact, if you cannot find happiness in this exact moment, then I promise you that no amount of money, no lifestyle change, no relationship, no award, and no life circumstance could ever bring you the happiness you seek. You need to take control of your life this instant and choose to become happy—and gratitude is the fastest and most tangible way to do that.

Clearly, the widely accepted practice of waiting for the latest, greatest thing to show up in our lives is simply not working. Now, I'm not saying we should abandon hope that "something better will come," or that the next job will pay more, or that the next home will be our dream home. It is appropriate and important to dream and hope. But...

There is a difference between always living in the future and hoping life will get better <u>someday</u> and beginning to live in the present and acknowledging that life is pretty great <u>right now.</u>

It is what Dieter F. Uchtdorf described as the difference between being thankful IN your current circumstances, whatever they may be, and being thankful FOR the things you can already acknowledge as "good" in your life.

By making gratitude an action—by *verbifying* it—we can begin experiencing gratitude, happiness, joy, fulfillment, and then we can begin taking control of *this* very moment.

By choosing to consciously DO gratitude regardless of our current circumstances, not only will we start to realize that we *already have* so many blessings, but we will also understand that our current circumstances, whether they are good or bad, act as the stepping-stones to the next amazing thing that is coming our way. To put it another way, I always tell my audiences:

I don't believe in failure.
In fact, I have never once experienced failure.
I only have stepping-stones to success.

It is the power of gratitude that instantly turns my perceived failure into a step forward in the evolution of becoming something awesome, as opposed to viewing my perceived failure as some negative or disappointing experience. Gratitude has the power to FLIP any perceived negative into something awesome.

With *active* gratitude, you can FLIP failure into success.
With *active* gratitude, you can FLIP hate into acceptance and love.
With *active* gratitude, you can FLIP hardship and challenge into endless opportunity.
With *active* gratitude, you can FLIP poverty and lack into prosperity and abundance.
With *active* gratitude, you can FLIP tragedy and loss into a richness of hope.

The process of FLIPping life's negatives into something incredible begins with a single decision. You must make a decision to examine the individual frustrations or challenges throughout the day, exactly in the moment that they come up, and decide that those minor trials are no longer going to dictate your mood or control your day.

You can have as many great days as you want to have. With the FLIP Formula, you are the one who gets to call the shots.

Life Happens
Let's go back to that Harris Poll for a minute. Why in the world are we SO unhappy? Why do we not experience more joy and contentment in life? And what is the cause of such a sweeping lack of joy?

My opinion? It's life. That's all — it's just life.

Life happens and will *always* be happening to us whether we want it to or not and life is full of challenges, difficulties, tragedies, mistakes, failures, and so much more.

I heard one of the greatest motivational speakers of all time, Les Brown, put it this way in a talk. "If it ain't one thing, it's twelve others. You will never ever have a problem-free moment in life. You're either in a problem, just left one, or headed toward one."

If you were to make a list of all the challenges you perceive yourself to be having this moment and in the past, can you imagine how depressing that would be? Obviously, creating such a list would not be healthy or helpful, and yet *that* form of thinking is the way most of us interact with life on a daily basis.

We love to focus on the bad.

It's almost as if we have somehow managed to bond together as human beings by comparing sob stories and communally complaining about our rotten, heaping piles of pointlessness.

Think of the statements you hear or say on a regular basis. Things like, "Gas has gotten so expensive." If gas is cheap at the moment, you'll still hear something like, "Yes, BUT, I remember when it was under a dollar."

It will *never* be cheap enough if you look at it that way.

You go to the movies and say, "They sure do gouge you on popcorn and soda." Yet, you buy it anyway, sulking at the money you are "throwing out the window."

A man I greatly admire named Joseph B. Wirthlin once put it like this:

> *"I believe that many people are unhappy because they have not learned to be grateful. Some carry the burden of bitterness and resentfulness for many years. Some pass their days as though suffering a deep sadness they cannot name. Others are unhappy because life didn't turn out the way they thought it would.*
>
> *"'If only I had money,' some might say to themselves, 'then I could be happy.'*
>
> *"'If only I were better looking.'*
>
> *"'If only I were smarter.'*
>
> *"'If only I had a new car, a college degree, a job, a wife, hair that wasn't so frizzy.' (Or, in my case, if only I had more hair or was twelve inches taller.)*
>
> *"If we only look around us, there are a thousand reasons for us not to be happy, and it is simplicity itself to blame our unhappiness on the things we lack in life. It doesn't take any talent at all to find them. The problem is, the more we focus on the things we don't have, the unhappier and more resentful we become."*

Life is coming at you whether you want it to or not. The phrase "if only" serves but one purpose—it keeps you from enjoying the life you have right now.

You know, today may very well be the absolute best day of your life. After all, you don't even know with 100% certainty whether you will wake up tomorrow! I hope to help you turn your "if only" mindset into an "I can't believe how good I've got it" outlook on the life you have RIGHT NOW.

Your New Super Power

If you consistently apply the FLIP Formula during key strategic moments throughout your day, I can guarantee that you will become happier and more fulfilled, and you can instantly regain control of your own life. I even have the science to prove it, and I will share it with you after we discuss the formula.

I love speaking to students. When I teach gratitude to students in junior high and high schools, I like to refer to active gratitude as their "super power." I do this for a few reasons, and let's use Captain America to illustrate:

Marvel's Captain America was given a special serum that transformed his levels of strength, endurance, agility, speed, reflexes, durability, and healing to superhuman levels — all helpful qualities when fighting bad guys, no doubt.

Well, what if "Cap" decided he didn't want to use his super powers? What if, despite all his super abilities and rippling abdominal muscles, he merely sat on the couch spooning some Ben and Jerry's?

He would not be considered a super hero if he never used the powers he was given.

Gratitude is the super power that has been given to you. If you only give gratitude a slight acknowledgement from time to time, you won't be "super" either. The power of gratitude can be harnessed when we spring into action and activate the inherent power stored in gratitude. You become super and change your world when you understand, use, and put active gratitude into practice.

I recently received an amazing message from a friend who had invited me to speak to a co-op group of homeschool parents and their students. Her eight-year-old son had really taken the simple and powerful message of FLIPping the Gratitude Switch to heart.

The day after I spoke, the boy surprised his mom with a note that read, "Mom, thank you for making food, comforting me, driving us places, and being nice. Love you." If that wasn't enough, I received another email a week later from my friend who recounted the following:

> *"Last night as I was laying with the kids in their room at bedtime, my eight year old said, 'Mom, I can't remember what 'I' means.' I had no idea what he was talking about, so I asked him what he meant. He said, 'Well, I remember what F and L stand for, but I can't remember what 'I' means.' He was going through (or attempting to go through) the FLIP process in his head.*
>
> *"Thankfully, my voice wasn't affected by the tears that started rolling down my cheeks as we laid there in the dark talking about the process you shared. I've tried to teach my kids to be grateful (we play the gratitude game and things like that), but FLIPping the Gratitude Switch is powerful!"*

I know how powerful this little FLIP can be for you, for your kids, and for the world, because I know how powerful it has been for me and my family.

I've watched FLIP change the lives of thousands of elementary and junior high school students and their counselors. I spoke at a large junior high, and the message of FLIP was so powerful that the counseling department decided to use the principles in this book as a continuing theme for the entire school year!

I've watched FLIP change the lives of high school students. The first high school that brought me into speak was an incredible school in Oregon. After the talk, I received this Facebook message from a sixteen-year-old female student:

> *"Hey! I just wanted to thank you for coming today and talking to our school. I know you had a good impact on a lot of us and definitely me in particular. Recently I went through an abusive relationship that carried on for almost a year in a half. It's only been a few months since the break up, but my heart has been over him for a long time. I was just too scared to leave.*
> *"I just wanted to say that you said something today that hit me hard, and I know I've been struggling with it, but I just didn't know how to deal. It was, 'Why be bitter when you could be thankful for the learning opportunity?' It really got me thinking that I need to use my experience in my past relationship as a learning and growing opportunity."*

I became emotional right away. What if this young lady's life could be changed forever because of one single FLIP? And what if she kept FLIPping every day?

I've seen entire company cultures shift by embracing and including the language of the FLIP Formula into the fabric of their company. I've seen adults weep with gratitude after attending talks I've given at organizations and boot camps. These incredible people became transformed by this simple principle and started incorporating it into their lives and homes immediately.

It is always so humbling and magnificent when someone applies these ideas, starts using the formula, and then tells me how it changed some aspect of their life. It makes ME so thankful that I was inspired to use gratitude, learn gratitude, and share it with others so that it will hopefully impact the world as much as it has impacted me.

And as I hope it will impact YOU.

Introducing the New Paradigm

What we are talking about here is far more than finding the silver linings in life's rain clouds. In fact, I take issue with that idiom. I'm making the case that there is no silver lining in a challenge… because the whole cloud is made of pure gold.

In the hustle and bustle of life and its many frustrations, let the following statement be the key to unlocking limitless joy and prosperity in your life:

> *It is the simple, daily, conscious decision to enact gratitude during the most frustrating times of the day—FLIPping The Gratitude Switch—that allows you to illuminate life's challenges, create more happiness, increase life fulfillment, drive more success, and ultimately deliver total control over all aspects of your life.*

Remember, when I began this journey, I was in a dark place. As soon as I started DOING gratitude rather than just feeling it, I discovered my hidden, internal switch. I felt so empowered—because no matter how big a frustration was, I had a mechanism to deal with it. I eventually gave that mechanism a name, a face, and ultimately assigned a process to it so that it was portable, simple, and easy to share with someone like you.

There are four simple steps to the FLIP Formula that will deliver everything you need. Once you learn them, you will be fully equipped to tackle any challenge, hardship, or frustration in your life going forward:

F = Find the Frustration

This first step is the act of recognizing and responding to frustrations as they arise throughout the course of your day. When something frustrating happens, acknowledge it, and realize you are being given the gift of initiating the FLIP Formula.

L = Look for What's Awesome

Now that you've located the frustration, isolate and analyze it for something awesome. In other words, find the good within the bad. Find the blessing embedded in the hardship, the joy embedded in despair, the success embedded in the failure. After a while, this search will become increasingly fruitful, as you begin to notice more and more things that you can consider amazing. Make a mental list of all of these incredible things hidden in that moment of frustration.

I = Initiate Gratitude

Now that you have located and isolated the frustration and found the good in the bad, you can choose to initiate or activate a process of gratitude for that hidden blessing. You take your list of what's awesome and go through it, mentally saying, "I'm so thankful for (fill in the blank)." THAT is what flips on the Gratitude Switch and THAT is the moment when everything changes. When you activate the power of gratitude by initiating your gratitude sequence, you are basically looking that frustration in the face and telling it, "Thank you for being my teacher."

P = Power up with #Gratifuel

Now that you have activated gratitude, you will feel changed inside. Warmer. Brighter. Less cynical. You will have sparked a chemical release of what's known as the "reward chemical," and your body will physically change, allowing the internal feeling you're experiencing to fuel you to the next frustration you encounter. That's when you rinse and repeat—again and again.

That is how you F - L - I - P the Gratitude Switch. Remember, it is through the simple, daily, conscious decision to activate gratitude during the most frustrating times of the day that you can change the entire trajectory of your life.

Are you ready to Find the Frustration, Look For the Awesome, Initiate Gratitude and Power-up With #Gratifuel? The next four chapters are dedicated to each one of the steps so that you can understand each part of the FLIP Formula more completely.

To download a one-page FLIP Formula Hot Sheet for a quick reference, visit FLIPTheGratitudeSwitch.com/CheatSheet

PART III

The FLIP Forumula

Now that you've seen the potential that exists by learning and using the active power of gratitude and FLIPping The Gratitude Switch in Part III, we will dissect and digest each step of the FLIP formula and, perhaps most importantly, learn how to start FLIPping the Gratitude Switch on a regular, consistent, and daily basis especially during life's most frustrating moments.

Chapter 1

F = Find the Frustration

My two sons *really* love dinosaurs. We play with them a lot in our home, and during our play, I've discovered something crazy. You may not know this, but not all of the dinosaurs are extinct. Yes! One species of dinosaur lives on.

Its name is the Notgoodenuffosaurus.

Notgoodenuffosaurus is a dinosaur that is more destructive than a hungry T-Rex, but it is found only in the unique climate created in the words you say and the thoughts you proliferate. Let me give you a list of some of the thoughts and words that create the perfect climate for the Notgoodenuffosaurus.

"I'm starving."
"I ate too much."
"This big house is so drafty."
"Our house isn't big enough to entertain."
"I'll never find my true love."
"I found love, but I wish they would change."
"It's too hot."
"I wish it were warmer."
"Could it BE any colder out there?"
"I hate driving in the rain."
"I just wish we could get some rain."
"There is not enough time."
"I'm too busy."
"My car isn't nice enough."
"New cars are so expensive these days."
"The dishwasher is loud."
"We don't even have a dishwasher."
"I don't really own my house—the bank does."
"Renting is so expensive."
"Food is so expensive."
"Healthy food is really expensive."
"They raised the prices on the value menu again."
"My spouse never acknowledged that nice thing I did."
"My spouse doesn't treat me the way I deserve to be treated."

"I have no control."
"It's not my fault."
"Republicans are idiots."
"Democrats are idiots."
"Why me?"
"It's not fair."

That list could go on for a long time, couldn't it? We could fill a library with books overflowing with negative feelings, statements of lack, and complaints.

Notice that a lot of the statements were different sides of the same coin, and yet both were negative statements. (It was too hot; now it's too cold). We tend to view the world through the Lenses of Limitation; we love to commiserate together over all the bad.

And misery loves company.

Maybe it *is* as Les Brown described it, and maybe we are either in a problem, getting out of one, or heading to the next one. Or maybe, just maybe, all of that stuff, all of those challenges are only "problems" because that is how we choose to *perceive* them.

Guess what? Here is the good news…

You don't have to view life in those terms! You **choose** to view life in those terms, which means that you can also choose a different, happier, more satisfying reality. You can make the Notgoodenuffosaurus become extinct by shifting the words you use to describe your life as you live it.

A Losing Argument

No matter what lens you choose, there is one certainty in life, and it is this: ***Throughout each and every day, you will inevitably encounter frustrations both big and small.*** What you may not know is that those seemingly little frustrations may culminate into the feeling that your entire life is headed in the wrong direction.

Most of the frustrations we deal with are minor occurrences that compound over time and lead us to believe that life is hard. When someone says, "I had such a bad day," did this feeling stem from some life-altering trouble? Maybe — but more often than not, this conclusion comes from the accumulation of multiple tiny frustrations. Here is how it normally works:

> You stub your toe getting out of bed, get frustrated, and feel the "anger monster" awaken in your gut, and as a result, snap at your spouse. Your son yells or your daughter complains, and you snap at your kids. Now the kids are crying, and your spouse is giving you the silent treatment. You limp into the bathroom, look in the mirror, and think, "I look terrible." As you declare your dissatisfaction with your reflection, you notice a new gray hair, and now you're livid. Oh, and you've only been up for ten minutes.

Or maybe your frustrations compound like this:

72

You go downstairs to discover you are out of milk, diapers, or toilet paper and your partner was the last one to use the item without replacing it. Rather than viewing it as small and insignificant, you go online and proclaim to Facebook, "Can't I catch a break already?" You then take a selfie with an exasperated look and post it on Instagram with the caption, "What a crappy Monday." Later that day, someone asks, "How are you?" and you reply, "To be honest, things could be better."

In either scenario, you are caught in an argument that is impossible to win... *You are in an argument with reality.* In one of my favorite books called *Loving What Is,* author Byron Katie says the following, "When [you] argue with reality, [you] lose — but only 100 percent of the time."

We've all heard that overused phrase, "It is what it is." Well, it's true! It actually IS what it is, and frankly, you can't do anything about it, because it already IS. What you CAN do is use a proven process like the FLIP Formula to deal with reality — with what already IS — and do some work on the internal turmoil you may be facing.

When you try to change what's already happened, it NEVER works. You can only change how you react to what's happened and what you do next.

Think of how often we express that something "should" have gone one way but didn't, or that something "could" have happened another way, but... it didn't. As long as we live in a state of perpetual dissatisfaction with what already IS, we can never really create the awesome reality we actually WANT.

We really do need to stop *shoulding* on ourselves.

I wonder what a verbal argument with reality would sound like? I imagine it would start like this, "Hey reality... I don't like your face!"

Okay fine, but that won't *change* reality's face. Reality's face will remain the same. You can close your eyes and not look at reality, or you can accept that its face is its face, and you can instead find something about that face that is attractive or pleasant in some way.

That's what the FLIP Formula can do! It can take you from frustration to liberation so that reality is not something to be argued with, but rather something to celebrate and feel gratitude for, regardless of what that reality looks like at any given moment.

The Driving Force Behind the FLIP

The power behind the FLIP Formula boils down to personal accountability — and that accountability starts by acknowledging frustration as soon as it shows up. You "find" the frustration by becoming present and aware of its existence, as opposed to letting it sweep you down the river of disappointment, at which point your only option is to climb out miles downriver dripping with discontent and wondering how in the world you got there.

The point of Finding the Frustration is to take a moment to acknowledge that a frustration exists, then to take that new acknowledgement and use it as a way to do some work on it. When a frustration, disappointment, or challenge arises, take a moment to become *aware* and *accountable.* Become aware of that feeling, and then become accountable by awakening to the fact that you have the power to change how you feel.

When the anger monster awakens, you must wake up and become conscious to the fact that something is rousing within. If you allow yourself to recognize the frustration, you can isolate that frustration and look at it with a degree of impartiality. When you find the frustration, acknowledge that it exists, and become aware that it is affecting you, and then you immediately create the power to do something about it.

I like to say that you give frustration a proverbial high five when it shows up and acknowledge it for what it is. Then, you take some simple actions in order to FLIP that frustration into something awesome through the power of active gratitude.

No Cord? ~~Big~~ No Problem!
In the midst of writing this book, I was scheduled to drive to Los Angeles for a marketing event and a mastermind group meeting. I booked the entire trip to last a week, cleverly giving myself some extra days after the meetings to feverishly work on my book—beautifully undisturbed—in my hotel room.

Upon arriving in LA, I had some time that evening before the first event started the following day, so I decided to spend a few minutes emitting *gratitude gold* onto my computer. I popped open my laptop, and there it was—my battery icon was glowing red and imploring, "Feed me." The battery was almost dead.

No problem, right? That's what power cords are for! Woefully, I quickly discovered that my power cord had not made the journey with me. It dawned on me that I was about to spend seven days of my life with no laptop on which to work, write, and constantly post how "grateful" I was on Facebook.

I was bugged. Really bugged. The hotel was already paid for, and I did NOT want to shell out another $85 for a Mac power cord (I already owned two of them, both sitting at home, probably mocking me). I began to conclude that I'd just head home after the events and abandon my brilliant plan to spend quality time on my book. This meant I was going to miss some deadlines, which made me even *more* frustrated.

I know there are people with real problems in the world, and this wasn't one of them. But allow me to dive into this frustration a little. I had already been working on this book for quite some time, and I had set deadlines in order to get the manuscript into the hands of the people who were helping me get it polished, edited, designed, and printed. My next deadline was just a few short days away. In fact, I was supposed to email the completed draft to my amazing writer friend Jen (shout-out to Jen) before I went back to Utah.

Now, Jen can tell you that deadlines and I don't exactly have a healthy relationship, especially not during the process of creating this book, but I really wanted to meet at least ONE deadline during the six months I'd *already* taken to write this book. I thought *this* might have been my one, quiet, perfect opportunity.

Nope.

As I sat there pondering my options, I picked up my phone, only to discover its battery was also on life support. Sadly, it was destined to die alongside my laptop since I had apparently also forgotten to pack my phone charger.

No phone, no laptop, no way to type anything.

How was I supposed to enter into the annals of nonfiction legend?

How could I create the scholarly version of Michelangelo's *David*?

Regardless of whether or not such a small problem *should* have been annoying and frustrating, I could not escape the fact that the predicament I was in was also completely and totally... my fault.

To make matters worse, the moment in which I discovered that I was regrettably cordless was at 11pm after an exhausting, thirteen-hour, traffic-laden drive. My blood sugar was also low due to the diet I was on at the time (to lose the spare tire I'd been sporting for the past few years).

It could have all stacked up to be one of those heart-wrenching, remote control throwing, wall kicking exclamations of frustration—but then I did the ONE THING I'm teaching *you* to do in this very book.
I took my own advice and put the FLIP Formula into action.

I could have chosen to let it all get to me. I could have also chosen to blame something or someone else for the situation. After all, my son Brody *had* been crying as I was packing my laptop bag that morning.

I could have SO easily shifted the burden of responsibility by saying, "If Brody hadn't cried, then I wouldn't have had to go change him. In fact, if my wife had been up at 6am, then she could have handled it, and I wouldn't have gotten distracted and forgotten the cord."

Blah, Blah, Blah.

That sounds a lot like Man #2 from "A Tale of Two Men," wouldn't you say? If I had become Man #2 in that moment, where would it have gotten me? Would it have changed the fact that the cords were not there? NO! Could the feelings of frustration and anger have powered up my computer and phone? NO! Would getting mad put me in a better state of mind to write a book on how to acquire unlimited happiness and control over your feelings? That's an unequivocal NO!

What does the choice to feel the frustration, anger,
and annoyance get anyone?
Absolutely nothing but anger, frustration, and annoyance.

It all boils down to a choice made in a single instant. I stopped and took an immediate inventory of my life. "I don't have the cord. I have a book to write… Okay." And that was all. I could either buy a new cord or accept that I wouldn't get any writing done on the trip.

It's that simple.

It simply is exactly *what it is,* so why fight it?

The process of becoming angry and arguing with reality is the *opposite* of what should be done when using the FLIP Formula. Becoming aware of the frustration, and then acknowledging and isolating it so you can go work on it and move past it in a healthy, productive way is how we can change our moments, our days, and ultimately our lives.

Small problems remain small.

Big problems are put into perspective.

And you get to stay happy, fueled by gratitude for every win and every struggle.

By the way, the conclusion of that story is actually pretty good. The next morning when I powered my drained iPhone back on, the remaining 8% of battery power was just enough to help me find an Apple Retail store a few miles away from my hotel. I went to the parking garage, hopped in my car and with my dangerously drained Apple iPhone battery, used the trusty GPS to navigate the busy streets of LA to the Apple Store, and arrived just before my 1% power turned into a black iPhone screen. I walked into the Apple Retail Store, and bought a new cord.

At first I thought it was my Gratitude Switch FLIPping, energetic, sparkling and hopelessly happy personality that prompted the Apple Store sales associate to tell me that within 15 days, I could return the power cord undamaged and with my original receipt, and get a full refund. I used the cord for the days I needed it and returned it no problem. I came to find out that apparently they give that return policy to all Apple customers; it was not my cheery disposition alone that prompted such stellar customer service. Nonetheless…Thank you Apple! (Dear Apple, I'm completely open to accepting any and all free Apple products you would like to ship to me as a way to show your gratitude for me sharing my amazing Apple story in this book. Sincerely, A Very Loyal and Happy Apple Customer).

Moments Create Lifetimes

Life is a collection of moments — good ones, bad ones, big ones, small ones, painful ones, and exquisite ones. And I propose that if life truly is nothing more than a collection of moments, it means you can change the trajectory of your life instantly by acknowledging how you show up for life in this exact moment.

FLIPping the Gratitude Switch allows us to determine the outcome of this life. It also allows you and me to more fully experience the splendor in beautiful moments, because gratitude illuminates everything. Because gratitude illuminates, it also allows us to navigate the dark times of life.

FLIPping The Gratitude Switch is the formula for never having a bad day again.

If you don't ever let another frustrating moment dictate your mood or your day, then that means you can compound all those moments that you FLIP and create an existence that is filled with joy, contentment, and happiness, an existence where you have total control of your mood, your day, and ultimately, your life.

You are the only one responsible for how you react to your reality! Even if situations arise over which you had no control, then you are still 100 percent responsible for how you choose to *react* and feel about the situation. And here's the best part: When you take responsibility for your frustrations (whether or not you were the cause), you gain control of them.

Would you rather choose to view life as a series of events where you are in control and can use the FLIP Formula to immediately experience significantly more joy, or do you forfeit control of your life as you sit and stew in self-pity and perceived victimhood?

I hope the answer is crystal clear.

Real Life Stuff

Let's take a look at a few other examples of the many tiny frustrations you may experience each day. I want you to become hyper aware of the tiny little *nothings* that are affecting *everything*. Here are some examples:

- You can't find a close parking spot.
- The soda pop machine is out of your favorite flavor.
- The vending machine ate a quarter and didn't give it back.
- There is such a long line at the bank.
- Your child does not make his or her bed when asked.
- There are dirty dishes piled up, but your spouse is firmly planted on the couch.
- The client you thought was a guaranteed buyer just fell through.
- Traffic... all of it.
- The price of gas went up again.
- Your DVR was set to record your favorite show, but it didn't record.
- Your favorite team lost.
- The toilet paper roll didn't get replaced, and you are staring (pants down) at the dreaded roll of empty cardboard.
- You burned the chicken because you got distracted making the salad.
- You trip over a cord.

I could go on all day, but hopefully you get the idea. It can be almost anything in the world, so long as it causes you the briefest moment of frustration.

Of course, there are big things too, and they absolutely cannot be overlooked. Traffic accidents can be big things. A terminal disease in you or a loved one is a major thing. Losing that loved one? That's even harder. Losing your job can also be life altering. The end of a relationship can be heartbreaking.

It can be *anything big or small* that is causing you pain or frustration.

While the primary purpose of this book is to teach you that the constant stream of daily frustrations is the largest root cause of most people's misery and dissatisfaction, if you haven't cultivated the practice of FLIPping The Gratitude Switch with the small things, it will be impossible to correctly use the FLIP Formula on the big things.

It is in those tiny moments of frustration where the seeds of anger are planted and the evolution of annoyance begins, and it is in those exact moments that the FLIP Formula and the process of FLIPping The Gratitude Switch can be the most impactful and powerful.

The small, almost unconscious reactions that we have each day to our micro-frustrations are what will determine our level of happiness and contentment, regardless of present circumstances. And, when you consciously choose gratitude, you consciously choose to create a happy life.

In order to master the FLIP, you first need to become proficient at being aware of the frustrating moments in life, even the tiniest ones, and as soon as you recognize them, alarm bells should go off in your mind, reminding you that it's time to FLIP the Gratitude Switch.

In each of life's moments, you are given the gift of choice—you can *choose* how to react. When you find the frustration in a moment and recognize it for what it is, it can become a beautiful gift, and it can become the foundation for the incredible, happy, and satisfying life you deserve.

Don't ignore those insignificant irritations. Acknowledge them, give them a high five, greet them with love, and realize you have some work to do. You don't have to live your life in a state of perpetual pessimism. You don't have to stay crouched and ready to battle the next problem waiting to ignite the moment you put out today's fire.

That's what step one is all about—*find a frustration* the moment it materializes and call it out. Once you find and acknowledge those frustrations, you get to start taking action on them! That action is introduced in the next step, which is called, "Look For What's Awesome."

And guess what? There is ALWAYS plenty of awesome.

Chapter 2

L = Look for what's Awesome

Getting a raise at work is awesome.
Someone did something nice for you? Also awesome.
You finally got that new car you wanted. Well, that's just awesome!

Feeling good about and having gratitude for things that are already awesome is important. But, it also doesn't require any effort — and it definitely doesn't require any sort of mental shift.

Popular activities like keeping gratitude journals, making gratitude jars, and going on gratitude walks are all good behaviors, and I encourage you to try such practices to see how they feel for you. Just be aware that the weakness with those approaches rests in the fact that they require you to give thanks for things that you ALREADY consider awesome.

FLIPping the Gratitude Switch requires you to look for what's awesome in your current circumstances, whatever they may be. This means that you must look for the good in things that, up until now, have done nothing but cause you irritation, grief, anger, or pain.

I know — it's a tough concept for some people to accept. There is an amazing story that perfectly illustrates the idea. It's a story about two sisters during World War II, as told by Nazi concentration camp survivor Corrie ten Boom. She and her sister, Betsie, were arrested and thrown into the notorious camp called Ravensbrück for helping hide Jews in the Netherlands during World War II.

In her book, *The Hiding Place,* Corrie recounted an amazing story of gratitude that paints one of the most beautiful pictures of finding the good within the bad that I have ever heard.

Soon after arriving at Ravensbrück, the women were horrified to discover that their living quarters, Barracks 28, was swarming with fleas. Upon discovering this, here was Corrie's response:

"Fleas!" I jumped down to the floor. "The place is crawling with fleas! I...I don't know how I can cope with living in such a terrible place!"

Her sister Betsie assured her sister that God had already given them the answer for how to handle the fleas, which was to give thanks without ceasing. She said to her sister:

"Come on, Corrie—let's try. What are we thankful for?"

Corrie did her best to list things she was grateful for—things like being able to hide her Bible from the guards and being together with her sister when other families had been totally separated. That's when Betsie added this:

"And thank you, God, for the fleas—"

Corrie thought her sister was crazy. There was no way she could ever be thankful for something as awful as fleas.

"No, Betsie! I can't thank God for the fleas. There's nothing good about them."
"Well, we'll just have to wait and see," my sister answered.

The women went out every morning at 4:30 A.M. to start their eleven-hour workday. They were fed just enough food to keep them breathing. The only thing they ever looked forward to was reading their smuggled Bible to the women in Barracks 28 at night. The sisters knew that they would be killed if the Bible got discovered, so they kept a watchful eye for guards every night during their reading. I'll let Corrie tell the rest of the story:

"But day after day passed, and no guards came into Barracks 28. Soon we read the Bible twice a day, and more and more women listened. No one bothered us. One day, Betsie grabbed my arm and whispered, "I know why no one has bothered our Bible studies. I overheard some of the guards talking. None of them wants to come into Barracks 28 because of the fleas!"
I wanted to laugh. "All right, Lord. Thank you for the fleas!"

It's truly an awe-inspiring story. Approaching gratitude in this way takes your gratitude game to the next level. When you DO find the awesome embedded IN the frustrations of life, it is significantly harder, which makes the practice of FLIPping The Gratitude Switch significantly more rewarding as a result.

The Awesome Needle in the Haystack of Frustration
In each moment that comes your way, both good and bad, you've got options; you really *do* have the power. YOU are the one who has the final say as to whether life is going to be painful, dull, and grey or joyful, exciting, and full of vibrant color.
Every formula is only as good as its next step. You can mix in the

flour, eggs, and butter, but if you don't put the mix in the oven, you won't be eating any brownies. Even though you may become really skilled at the first step of the FLIP Formula, the whole recipe hinges on the next step. The Gratitude Switch cannot be FLIPped until you look for what's awesome!

We are going to do a few practice runs at finding the awesome. In them, I will show you how to take a frustration and find the good. And guess what? There's always good.

So how does this work? It's pretty straightforward. After we acknowledge and isolate any frustration, we must find some way that the annoyance, trial, or tribulation is awesome, and even a blessing—just like how the fleas (normally a giant, painful nuisance) became a blessing for Corrie and Betsie.

It is in this step that you begin to physically FLIP that Gratitude Switch.

Let's take a look at some of the items from the list of the daily hardships in the last chapter. These were some of the everyday experiences that may be affecting our day without our knowledge or permission. We are going to call them out and then dissect them to discover the shards of awesome embedded within each one.

Any one of these common occurrences could cast a pall on the entire day and trigger a negative ripple effect that reaches not just your day, but also the days of your family, friends, and co-workers. That is why, when you take the moment after you find the frustration to discover what is *awesome*, you effectively begin charting a new course for your mood, your day, and your life:

You can't find a close parking spot.

This one happens to all of us at some point. Really, you've just been handed a great opportunity to burn a few extra calories. Even better, next time, don't *look* for a spot close to the building. Instead, make a conscious decision to park further away! Get out of your car and start walking with a purpose, thinking about how amazing it is that you can fit a few more steps into your day and give your heart and legs a mini workout.

Awesomehood achieved!

The soda machine is out of your favorite flavor.

I used to love root beer as a kid. But at some point in life, we grow up and move on to more *mature* drinks like Mountain Dew and Diet Coke. Well, if that machine is out of Diet Coke, consider this your inner child's way of telling you that it wants root beer. You might even experience a little nostalgia as you take that first sip.

This could also be an opportunity to step outside your soda pop comfort zone and try a new flavor. Who knows? You may discover a new favorite. Better yet, opt for a bottle of water and realize how remarkable it is that life handed you a reminder to be healthier.

Lastly, maybe the real awesome is that you live in a world that allows you to place little pieces of metal into a machine that dispenses refreshment. What a blessing that you have enough pieces of metal money to buy a drink in the first place. That's more than many folks have.

Awesomesauce discovered!

There is a long line at the bank.

This is a tough one for me at times. I have to remind myself that I am a business owner, an entrepreneur, and someone who really believes in free market principles. And because of that, I always love it when I see someone who has a job. Businesses can't hire if they are not profitable. If businesses don't have customers, then they have no way to turn a profit. If there is a long line at the bank, then I just think of how awesome it is that the establishment has so many customers, because it means that more money is being made and injected into society, which means that more jobs have been created, which means that more families are able to provide for themselves. I'm good with that.

All of a sudden, a long line turns from a source of frustration into a symbol of prosperity, and I feel great that I have enough prosperity to either deposit the check I have in my hand or take cash out. Not only is the business profitable, but I am as well.

You have just been Awesomed!

You child does not make his or her bed when asked.

The first and most obvious awe-inspiring newsflash... you have kids! What a blessing! It can be so easy to let the daily grind of parenthood become fraught with frustration. Sometimes it may feel hard to look for the good embedded in that parental mayhem.

You have children, and they are alive and have the ability to make their bed, regardless of whether they do it when asked. I think of all the friends who have lost children or haven't been able to have children, and I think about family or friends who have amazing special needs children who won't ever be able to make their own beds. When I think of them, I instantly realize how blessed my wife and I are to have healthy, able-bodied kids.

When cooler heads prevail, and you can communicate clearly and calmly with your children to help them understand why it helps the family to have them make their bed, they are significantly more likely to eventually do it. In my experience, when I stew in the frustration and lash out, my kids rarely ever fix the behavior in question. Be cool—the fact that you have a home and beds for your kids is reason enough to celebrate.

Mr. and Mrs. Awesome, your table is ready. Please follow me!

There are dirty dishes in the sink, but your spouse is firmly planted on the couch.

My wife can relate to this one since that was I (the firmly planted one) for many years. I consider this often, because we have had the ability, even during the lean times, to abundantly feed our children. They have never been hungry a day in their lives. That line of thought is so encouraging to me and causes me to reflect on how many do not have that ability. Yes, there are dishes to do, but only because we have been fed. When you think of it that way, it becomes easy to brush off frustration about a few plates and forks.

If you are struggling with your spouse sitting firmly on the coach engrossed in the game instead of doing the dishes, my wife could offer you some insight on that one. She might say something like, "How awesome is it that he works hard for our family to put food on the table, and now he is bonding with the kids while watching the 49ers game."

The representative from the nation of Awesome has the floor!

The big deal (that was "guaranteed") just fell through.

If you are in any kind of sales position (and we all are, really), this one has happened. If it hasn't, then it will at some point. There is always a client that you invest a ton of time in that ends up going elsewhere or not buying at all. This client may have assured you 100 times that they are sticking with you, but then something happens—and they don't.

How could this possibly be awesome? For years, I've conditioned myself to believe that each *no* I receive brings me one step closer to a *yes*. So, if I get a *no* (and even if it came after investing a lot of my personal time), I get excited, because I just took a big step towards my next *yes*.

I also get an opportunity to reflect on what I could have done better during the sales process. Learning is so valuable, and I relish any opportunity to learn. Perhaps I can identify at what point in the process I should have helped the client take action, and now I can fix that going forward and improve my closing ratio in the future.

Have you heard this new group called The Awesomes? They are AWESOME!

Traffic... all of it.

I moved to Utah in 2001, leaving behind the traffic soaked freeways of the San Francisco Bay Area, and as a result, I have now become traffic spoiled. There is rarely traffic in Utah—but when there *is* traffic, I still have to battle my inclination to have a mild conniption fit.

When I drive to Los Angeles, a ten-hour drive often turns into a thir-teen-hour drive because of traffic. At times, the interstates around LA basically become a parking lot. In the past, I have acted like many others who I have seen exit their cars and throw their hands up in pure exasperation.

I have now learned to view traffic as purely awesome because it allows me to spend extra time in a climate-controlled vehicle where I can listen to books, podcasts, scriptures, and music. Many people complain that their hectic pace rarely gives them the opportunity to take a step back and have some time to themselves. Well, traffic does just that! If I get even one new idea from a book I am listening to while sitting in traffic, it's all worth it.

If traffic makes me late, I remind myself that traffic didn't make me late; I made me late by not anticipating the traffic and leaving early enough. It becomes a great lesson on the importance of punctuality.

I also find the awesome in the fact that I have a car I can trust not to overheat in traffic (that is something that used to happen to me in college). By the way, don't forget that being stuck in traffic means that you have the ability to drive a car at all.

That comes in two shades, Awesome, and Really Awesome!

The price of gas went up again.

Sometimes, gas can get expensive. Pause for a moment and think about the feeling that something is "expensive." What does that indicate? First of all, it is a clear sign that you have money. If you have no money, it's not expensive; it's just plain impossible.

When gas increases in price, you notice because you've been buying gas. That means you have a car AND you can actually afford to put gas in it! There are many millions in this world who could never even consider such a thing.

If you are frustrated with the price of gas because you remember back when it cost less, this means you've owned a car for a while now. You get to enjoy a luxury that the majority of the world will never experience.

And consider this: You actually *have access* to gasoline. You can drive up to a little pump and fuel up the vehicle that takes you to your job, to church, and to the kids' play dates or sports practice. So, the awesome comes through the blessing of access.

Prices go up and down. It's supply and demand. And yes, many prices go up and never come back down (like admission prices to Disneyland). I can guarantee that many will be frustrated by such increases. What a luxury to be frustrated with such a small thing! If you are frustrated by the price increase of a Disneyland Park Pass, for example, it means you have the ability to go, or even the ability to consider going to an amusement park. Prosperity is a state of mind — and it's a state of mind you choose!

What's the wait time for Awesome Mountain? There's no line? AWESOME!

Your team lost.

My wife will tell you that she has seen me become absolutely en-raged when my favorite pro or college team lost to their arch rival. This one should be a no brainer. I have had the luxury to be raised in a country where so many professional sporting events take place, and thanks to technology, I've been able to watch and track these teams.

There will always be other games, other seasons, and other cham-pionships. These days, I simply sit back, root for my team, and let a loss or a frustration melt away, realizing how awesome it is that I could even experience the game in the first place. I get mad, I react, maybe make a few comments on what I wish the team would have done better, but then take a deep breath, and just let the gratitude flow with the hope and thought that the next game or season is just around the corner.

Final Score In Overtime: One Hundred and Awesome
To One Hundred and Awesome. Awesome Wins!!

Awesome Ain't Always Easy

My hope is that the awesome found in each of those situations got you thinking about how you can program your thought process to work. As with anything worthwhile in life, it will take some practice, and if you've been practicing negative speak for many decades, the change may not hap-pen overnight. All you can do is actively choose to use the FLIP Formula when you find yourself facing one of the many inevitable daily frustrations awaiting us all.

Last year I had just given a talk to a group of parents and students, and an older woman approached me. She did not look like she fit with the audience I had spoken to (young kids and their parents), so I wondered why she was there.

It turns out she had heard a podcast interview about *FLIP The Grat-itude Switch,* and she had researched me online and read most of my blog posts. When she discovered I would be speaking near her town, she drove to see me.

She showed up to ask me a really tough question.

Her terminally ill mother's home had recently burned down. The woman was now battling on behalf of her mother with multiple insurance companies—both the medical side and homeowner's side—because she felt the insurance companies were doing everything in their power to avoid pay-ing the claims.

This woman was beside herself. She was finding it next to impossible to FLIP the Gratitude Switch and look for something awesome within these major challenges. I offered a few ways that she might find some awesome. I started by saying, "Wow, I'm so sorry you are going through that! Let me see if I can help. Can you find the good in the fact that your mom has insurance at all?"

She shook her head. "No, because the insurance companies aren't doing anything."

Strike One.

I tried again. "Well, can you find some good in the idea that your mother will eventually get a newly built home out of this terrible trial?"

She frowned. "I don't think we will, because the insurance company is not working with us. Besides, she lives in a condo."

Strike Two.

I was not going to be deterred. "I know your mother is in pain, and it seems like things aren't going well, but let me ask you this: Do you love her? And will you miss her when she's gone?"

She solemnly replied, "Well, of course I love her, and I will miss her."

"Then take advantage of every second of every day that you have left with her. The other stuff stinks, and it will eventually work itself out. But in the meantime, can you try to be thankful for the moments you DO get with her?"

"Yeah, I guess I can."

That brief conversation taught me a powerful lesson. Sometimes we can't control the big stuff; things just happen. What we can control are the little moments surrounding the big stuff. We can find little moments to be thankful and to discover the awesome in some aspect of our life at the moment that the big stuff is happening.

When you can become thankful in your current circumstances, and when you practice FLIPping the Gratitude Switch consistently and regularly, you will become addicted to doing it for everything. That is when the big stuff somehow becomes easier to handle. The gravity of serious situations does not get diminished, but your capacity to interact with those situations and deal with them will improve drastically.

Remember, it is through the simple, daily conscious act of finding the frustration then looking for what's awesome that begins to lay the foundation for an entirely new way of looking at life.

The list of what's awesome doesn't need to be written down. You can do it all in your head. Once you've obtained your list of the good, you will immediately move to the third step of the FLIP Formula, where you take that list and do something really powerful with it—it is where you complete your verbification of gratitude.

So, how do we initiate the gratitude sequence with our mental list of awesome, and do it in a way that will actually cause a real, lasting, and powerful internal shift? That leads us to the third step of the FLIP Formula, "Initiate Gratitude." We must actually initiate, activate, and then *experience* the quiet power of "thank you" in our hearts.

Chapter 3

I = Initiate Gratitude

Have you ever considered how a world-class runner like Usain Bolt wins the 100-meter dash? Sure, there are years of preparation and practice and untold hours of running. But lots of people do those things and still never win Gold medals. So how does he actually win?

He crosses the finish line first.

I know that seems like an oversimplification, but consider this for a moment. There is an instant in Usain Bolt's life when some part of his body physically crosses the finish line first that makes him the winner.

Everything that came before laid the foundation for and contributed to his ability to win, but that single moment where he exerts the final bit of effort to cross the line *first* is arguably what counts the most.

What if Usain Bolt put in all those years of preparation and the untold hours of mechanics and practice, BUT just one yard short of the finish line during the Olympics medal winning race, he decides to stop running?

Does he still become a champion? Of course not.

The One Millisecond That Makes You A Champion

For Usain Bolt, all the preparation and work in the world becomes pointless if he doesn't push all the way to that last millisecond when he crosses the finish line first.

This is analogous to your life after this book.

If you want to win in life, you can't stop just short of the finish line.

The difference is we aren't talking about a single win. We are talking about your participation in the arena of life, where every day can be a triumph. Each moment of each day truly can be a victory if you *choose* for it to be. Notice the importance of the word *choose* — you must *choose* to win, or you never will.

Which leads us into the third part of the FLIP Formula, initiating gratitude. This third step is where your mind and body start to become something different. It's the home stretch on the way to the figurative Gold medal. The practice of *initiating gratitude* is what will flood your life with the light of possibility and hope — and what ultimately leaves you victorious.

It is also here that the symbolic FLIPping of the Gratitude Switch takes place.

At this point in the formula, you've run a solid race so far. You found and isolated the frustrations, and then you looked for and found the awesome in each one—but the work is not over yet.

Think of it this way: Let's say you walked into a large dark room that held the key to your happiness somewhere within its obscured reaches. You reached your hand out to flip on the light switch, but at the last moment, you chose not to flip it. Instead, you remain shrouded in darkness, destined to walk around bumping into walls and complaining about how impossible it is to navigate the room in the dark.

You did everything necessary to bring you to that point in your life, but with your hand on the switch that holds the key to a better future, you choose not to exert that final bit of effort to illuminate the task and make everything, brighter, better, and easier.

It's the same as finding all the frustrations in your day, looking for what's awesome in them, but then stopping dead in your tracks. If you decide that the race ends there, you are missing that one small, yet significant action that will enable your circumstances to change and allow you to become a champion every day.

But what if, after you found the frustrations and looked for the awesome, you put your hand on that switch, and then chose to exert the tiniest bit more effort to flip it? The room would be flooded with light, your route would be illuminated, and your success virtually guaranteed.

Step three is the critical FLIP of the switch that turns gratitude from some "thing" into an action that will flood your day with life-giving light. In other words, this is the point at which you finalize your VERBIFICATION of gratitude by physically expressing thanks.

Eyes Wide Open

The tangible *experience* of gratitude is what makes all the difference. Without it, you are merely feeling thankful rather than participating in the full spectrum and glorious warmth of gratitude.

Here is how step three works: Once you choose to flip the metaphorical switch, you begin to look around with your eyes open. After all, all the light in the world won't do you any good if you keep your eyes shut.

It's important to note that we aren't talking about scanning your surroundings—you must look around *internally*. Your heart needs to receive the awesome you found in step two and disseminate that recognition (and the feeling that accompanies it) throughout your body.

You take action on your list of awesome by triggering your body to literally *feel* the gratitude.

There is a big difference between saying "Thank you" and initiating and feeling gratitude. It's the kind of gratitude that Hal Elrod—author of the international bestseller, *The Miracle Morning,* and author of this book's foreword—calls "soulful gratitude." Soulful gratitude is a real, tangible emotion that you can feel well up inside of you.

It's a significantly more involved process than just thinking about being thankful.

Soulful gratitude does not happen by accident. It takes conscious effort and a mindful application of the FLIP Formula. After you find a frustration and look for what's awesome, you now have a list of things to be thankful for embedded inside any number of frustrations. By creating that list, you are essentially choosing to feel gratitude rather than experience the typical annoyance about one of life's frustrations.

The frustration is still there, but because you found the awesome in it, you are in essence feeling gratitude for the frustration itself.

This process of initiating soulful gratitude is truly powerful and life altering.

As I mentioned in the last chapter, finding the awesome embedded within the frustrations of life is significantly harder — and that fact makes the practice of FLIPping the Gratitude Switch significantly more rewarding as a result.

Why? Because you get stronger when you do harder things.

In the same way your muscles grow stronger by lifting heavier weights, you are strengthening your gratitude muscles when you express gratitude for frustrations after you have located the awesome embedded in those frustrations.

Anyone can say "thanks." In fact, "Thank you" has become a lot like, "I'm sorry" or the typical greeting, "How are you?" Sometimes, we really mean these things; other times, we say them out of obligation or habit.

Saying the words "thank you" can never a bad thing. But that alone does not make you a grateful person. *Soulful gratitude, on the other hand, is the act of triggering real emotional gratitude that causes your soul to stir.* The only way to trigger the eternal power of gratitude is to initiate it and feel it, and then express it outwardly by feeling it as you express it.

You need to *feel* the words, not just say them.

Why Thanksgiving Stinks

Thanksgiving is about "thanks" right? I mean, come on; it's built right into the name. But when was the last time you really felt gratitude for each bite of turkey? As you shovel potatoes and gravy down your throat, do you think of those who have no food at all, much less a feast? As you devour a second slice of pumpkin pie, do you feel gratefulness wash over you as you realize how blessed you are in that exact moment?

Thanksgiving has become a day when we merely give lip service to gratitude — and then there's the day *after* Thanksgiving. I'm always amazed by Black Friday, except now there is barely even a Black Friday anymore; now it is more like a shadowy Thursday. Now, before our food has even had time to digest, even before the tryptophan and food coma has time kick in, we race out to scoop up doorbuster deals before our neighbor can. Our meal of thanks has been converted to a delicious placeholder, as a way take up time before we can head out to "beat the crowds." Selfishness tends to be the prevailing emotion, which is ironic since real gratitude breeds humility and tends to root out ego and selfishness.

I can't fault the retailers. They are merely responding to the demands of the consumer. The problem here goes much deeper: *There is a staggering lack of gratitude on a day dedicated to the giving of thanks.*

I like giving and receiving a good present on Christmas as much as the next guy, but should getting the deal really become more important than spending time with family on the day that is supposed to be dedicated to expressing gratitude for our families?

"Dinner was delicious, honey. But now I gotta go body check an old lady so I can save $100 on a flat screen TV. Save me some pumpkin pie, because saving money, and yummy food is WAY more important than the relationship we share. Bye!"

Many families I know scatter out like hyenas to forage for the best deals at multiple stores. They leave other family members at home as they venture out to spend money they don't have on things they don't need, all while sacrificing precious time with the most important people in their world.

Even when we do stay home, we eat as quickly as possible so we don't miss the big game. We spend our time complaining about an annoying family member or the pie that didn't turn out right. The kids whine about the food taking too long while we complain that our team isn't playing well. Or we peruse the Black Friday ads, all while we neglect the real sense of gratitude we ought to be having for our family and for the abundance in which we get to partake.

You are not thankful or truly experiencing gratitude simply because you are celebrating a day that has the word "thanks" in it. You are only truly thankful when you take a moment to initiate, and feel, I mean really feel gratitude for the gifts of family and abundance.

A Mini Gratitude Experiment

Allow me to show you how profound the difference can be between expressing gratitude and initiating and feeling gratitude. Go into your bathroom look at the mirror. That's right—walk in there, stare into your gorgeous eyes, and say the following words: "Thank you."

I'll wait here…

So, how'd it go? Did you feel good when you did it? I imagine it felt significantly better than if you looked in the mirror and said, "Forget you, weirdo."

And now, I want you to feel and experience more than just a simple thank you. So, go back to your mirror and do three things:

1. Look at yourself and consider how lucky you are to have a body that allows you to step up to the mirror and utter any words at all.

Realize that many don't have such a gift—but you do. Become aware of your ability to perform this task by thinking of someone (a loved one who has passed, perhaps) who does not have that blessing.

2. Close your eyes and think of something that brings you joy, more joy than anything else in the world. I like to visualize my wife and children embracing me in a group hug, as we all say in unison, "Family hug!" Whatever it is for you—a warm beach, a good meal, your favorite spot in the forest—close your eyes and go there. Take a moment and feel how awesome it is to be there. Let that warmth and goodness wash over you.

3. Open your eyes and look once more at your marvelous body as you think of your happy place or idea. Now look yourself in the eyes again, and say audibly and with emotion, "Thank You!"

I can't know what your reaction was, or even if you conducted this little experiment, but if you did, I will bet you a shiny nickel that the second "Thank You" felt different from the first one. What you experienced the second time is how you initiate and express gratitude in a genuine, tangible, and lasting way.

True Gratitude Must Be Actionable

In the book-turned-phenomenon known as *The Secret,* there is a practice that is described as "vision boarding." It is the idea of making a board filled with pictures of things that you hope to have in your life. Then you put that board somewhere where you will see it often. This practice is supposed to activate the Law of Attraction and, in theory, begin to bring those things you want into your life.

Although vision boarding can work, it is something that only works if you do more than stare at pictures all day. If all you do is look at a board without taking any action, then the power of the practice can never actually be activated.

John Assaraf is a successful businessman in many ways, but he is perhaps best known for a story he shared in *The Secret,* specifically about his personal experience with using a vision board. Here is an excerpt:

"I was getting ready to move. We put all the furniture, all the boxes, into storage, and I made three different moves over a period of five years. And then I ended up in California and bought this house, renovated it for a year, and then had all the stuff brought from my former home five years earlier.

"One morning my son Keenan came into my office, and one of the boxes that was sealed for five years was right at the doorstep. He asked, 'What's in the boxes, Daddy?' And I said, 'Those are my Vision Boards.'

"He then asked, 'What's a Vision Board?' I said, 'Well, it's where I put all my goals up. I cut them out and I put all my goals up as something that

I want to achieve in my life.' Of course at five and a half years old he didn't understand, and so I said, 'Sweetheart, let me just show you, that'll be the easiest way to do it.'

"I cut the box open, and on one Vision Board was a picture of a home that I was visualizing five years earlier. What was shocking was that we were living in that house. Not a house like it – I actually bought my dream home, renovated it, and didn't even know it. I looked at that house and I started to cry, because I was just blown away. Keenan asked, 'Why are you crying?' 'I finally understand how the law of attraction works. I finally understand the power of visualization. I finally understand everything that I've read, everything that I've worked with my whole life, the way I've built companies. It worked for my home as well, and I bought our dream home and didn't even know it."

I had the privilege of meeting with John at the home he talks about in *The Secret*. He showed that original vision board to the group of us having dinner in his home. As we examined it, he told us, "That moment [pulling the board out of the box] was one of the greatest epiphanies of my life because up until that time, there wasn't any scientific evidence; there wasn't any explanation for how miracles happen. But I knew that with the research I'd done on quantum physics, on quantum mechanics and the brain, I finally put all the pieces together. There is some magical amazing power that is emanating from our brains and our thoughts."

As a looked at the board, it became clear to me how John had achieved this remarkable feat. He didn't just look at the board on occasion; it wasn't an office accessory; he would look at his board and quite literally experience what it was like to already be in that home.

Even then, his work did not end there.

Each day he would work as hard as possible, doing the required – and the unrequired – work to achieve success. All the while, he continued to look at the board and feel as though he already owned the home. That daily effort manifested itself into the home in which I was now standing.

There was a tremendous amount of action that went into his accomplishment. After spending time with John, it became clear that he is a man who passionately goes after what he wants. He works hard in order to achieve extraordinary results and maintain extraordinary results.

The keys to John's success were his visualization techniques, and perhaps more importantly, his action. He didn't just sit around with his eyes closed, imagining what it would be like to live in that house. He got up and did something in order to move him closer to actually arriving at his desired destination.

Wake Up and Activate!

Remember, if gratitude is a verb, then it is actionable. Every part of the FLIP Formula is actionable, which means that it requires some sort of conscious effort on your part. Finding and isolating the frustration is an active process; looking for and locating the awesome is also an active process.

The third part of the formula—initiating and *feeling the gratitude*—is equally actionable. And I have found that one of the best ways to make feeling gratitude actionable is to actually *do* something to express it.

Recognizing this a few years ago, I began practicing something that truly changed my life—every morning I choose to receive the gift of FLIP-ping the Gratitude Switch the moment I wake up.

I set my alarm for 5am most weekdays, and as soon as that alarm sounds, I look at the clock and do a quick calculation of how long I slept. Then, I immediately choose to FLIP the Gratitude Switch as opposed to giving into the more common feeling that prevails at 5am, which is "I'm so tired."

Instead, I tell myself, "Wow, six (or four or five) hours was EXACT-LY the amount of sleep I needed to feel good and be successful today."

I take a moment and let that feeling of gratitude wash over me, and then I say out loud, looking upwards, "Thank you." I start my day with a victory. I'm victorious for getting up, and I'm victorious because the first choice I made and the first action I took was gratitude.

More than just saying those words, I'm saying them to some-body—I'm saying them to God. It is my belief that this glorious life of mine is a gift from God. When I say "thank you" to Him, I feel the gratitude because I truly mean it. I am soulfully thankful for the gift of life, breath, family, forgiveness, repentance, and health. That expression, combined with the initiation of an emotional gratitude sequence, allows me to start each day with a powerful chemical release in my body (as you will see in the next chapter) that will make every day an extraordinary one.

Exercising gratitude first thing in the morning will help you set the right tone for the entire day—and it doesn't have to take more than a few seconds. When you practice the FLIP Formula regularly, you will learn to execute all of the steps in less time than it used to take you to grumble about being tired as you stumble into the bathroom.

Exercise Your FLIP Muscles

I remember going to the archery range for the first time in Boy Scouts and thinking that archery should be really easy because it *looked* so easy when others did it. I excitedly picked up the bow and began to pull, but I could barely budge the string back an inch. But I kept pulling, and all of a sudden, it got past a certain point and could be easily pulled back the rest of the way.

The more I practiced drawing back the bowstring, the easier it be-came. I remember my Scout leader explaining that the reason it is so difficult in the beginning is because you use a different set of muscles to pull back a bowstring than the muscles you typically use outside of archery. He then told us a story to reinforce his point:

"One day while practicing at an indoor archery range and store, I saw

"an extremely muscular man walk into buy a compound bow. He looked at the bows and pointed to a really good-looking one on the wall."

"The nice woman behind the counter was quite small. She eyeballed the muscled man, looked back at the bow he was pointing to, and asked him, "Sir, how often do you shoot?""

"He replied that it was his first time to go bow hunting. In fact, he hadn't shot many bows before, but he felt confident that he needed the biggest, strongest bow they offered. The woman responded by saying, "Okay sir, then I don't think this bow will be for you. I think its draw weight might be a little heavy.""

"The man was obviously incensed and arrogantly waved her off, responding that she should just hand him the bow. She shrugged, "Okay, I only mentioned it because this bow is a 60-pound bow, which one of the heavier pulls men use.""

"The man snickered. "Gimme a break — 60 pounds? I think I'll be just fine.""

"She shrugged and handed him the bow. He picked it up, put his fingers on the string, and began trying to draw it back. He was unable to budge it more than a few inches before he set it down on the counter and barked, "You must have given me the wrong one. This can't be 60 pounds. I can hardly pull it back.""

"Without saying a word, the woman picked the bow up off the counter, held it up, and drew the string back all the way in one seamless, effortless movement. She then used her 105-pound frame to hand the bow back to the man. "No, it's the right one. That definitely feels like 60 pounds.""

"The muscle man left the store completely embarrassed."

This story illustrates a powerful point for our discussion here. FLIP-ping the Gratitude Switch is going to feel foreign at first, and maybe even fairly difficult if you are not someone who often employs an attitude of gratitude on a regular basis.

Even if you feel that you are a pretty thankful person, successfully using the four-part FLIP Formula will take some practice. But while it may feel like a little bit of a struggle, over time, it will become much easier. Consider it an exercise of your "gratitude muscles."

If that is true—if we are exercising some new muscles—doesn't it make sense that we need to perform some physical exercises? After all, those muscles ain't gonna grow themselves.

We need action, which is what step three in the FLIP Formula is all about. After you feel gratitude and become good at exercising your gratitude muscles, you still need to *express* the gratitude. It helps to have some sort of physical act to remind you of the process you just went through and the feelings you can now experience.

The expression can be simple. It can be an audible utterance of "thank you," much like what you did during the experiment earlier in the chapter or like I do in my early morning routine.

What is nice about expressing gratitude in this way is it can be done anywhere and anytime—you are not reliant on having a pen and journal nearby at all times.

I like to post about my FLIPs and feelings of gratitude on social media as a way of holding myself accountable for FLIPping. It also allows others to experience the gratitude with me. Perhaps my favorite way to physically express gratitude is to say a small, simple prayer of thanks. Hearing the words aloud or in my head makes it all so real—so tangible.

Taking those brief seconds to feel the soulful gratitude will act as the bonding agent in the FLIP Formula and the process of FLIPping the Gratitude Switch.

We All Need a Little Reminding

When I started to apply the principles in this book, I found myself searching for a physical reminder of how simple and powerful it can be to FLIP The Gratitude Switch. I also wanted a simple way to teach my children about the power of learning to FLIP The Gratitude Switch. Sometimes, we already know what we know, but we just need a little nudge to use what we know.

That is when I created a special object that serves as an ever-present reminder of the importance of physically FLIPping the Gratitude Switch during life's frustrating moments.

It is a simple light switch cover imprinted with the words:
"FLIP THE GRATITUDE SWITCH."

The light switch's message is a command that I see multiple times a day. I put the first one I ever made in my bathroom, and each time I flip that switch, I read the words on the light switch plate and interpret it as a call to action in that very moment. When I actually flip the switch, the room is flooded with light, just like when I FLIP The Gratitude Switch and my life is flooded with the fulfilling joy of love and gratitude.

Next, I put one in my daughter's room. My daughter was five years old when I began teaching her how to FLIP the Gratitude Switch. Even at such a young age, she has received it well and seems to understand the power and simplicity of the FLIP Formula.

Before we gave our daughter her own switch, one evening, I asked her to clean her room, and she *really* did not want to. She stood looking at me defiantly, but then all of a sudden, she said, "One second…" Then she turned around and walked down the hall.

I called after her, trying to figure out what she was thinking. She walked down the hall and flipped on the bathroom light. Then she came back down the hall and said, "Okay, now I'm ready." She went to work and did what I asked her to do.

As she was cleaning up her room, I asked my daughter, "Sweetheart, why did you go down the hall when I asked you to clean up your room?"

She said, "Dad, I didn't really want to clean up my room, so I just had to go FLIP The Gratitude Switch real quick so I could be thankful I have a room."

It was pure bliss as a father.

I have realized that it is through the simple, conscious, and physical internal practice of FLIPping my Gratitude Switch that my happiness levels have increased immensely. I go through the formula every time I feel the slightest anger or frustration start to surface. It has become a part of my entire family's daily routine. I have practiced the FLIP Formula so often that I rarely have to think through each step.

It has become habit, and I'm addicted to it in a really good way.

I created the light switch covers to help you work your gratitude muscles and also to make it as easy as possible to start incorporating the powerful process of FLIPping the Gratitude Switch in your life. I'm not alone in this thinking.

As I travel across the country sharing this message and my light switch plates with audiences both young and old, I've had hosts of parents tell me how powerful it is to have a Gratitude Switch in their home. One dad told me, "The light switch cover alone has *completely* shifted the way my children act at home. Thank you, thank you, thank you!"

One of my favorite examples of how effective the light switch plate has been for a family was from a courageous, single mother of 4, she said, "I have my kids go into a dark room and 'FLIP the Gratitude Switch,' and I love the powerful image when they do—the darkness is dispelled! The light forces the darkness out! They can see it!"

To claim your own free FLIP light switch plate, please visit:

FREEGiftFromKevin.com

Having your own light switch cover in your home or office (or both) will serve as a constant reminder of how easy it can be to not only increase your happiness and contentment levels, but also how frequently you should FLIP the Gratitude Switch in your life.

So, let's do a quick recap. At this point in the FLIP Formula, you've done three things:
1) You found the frustration.
2) You looked for what's awesome within the frustration.
3) You initiated gratefulness in some physical way (a simple internal or external action), thus enabling your body and your spirit to become active participants in the gratitude.

Now that you know how to enact gratitude in your life, let's explore how it can fill you up and fuel every aspect of your life by exploring the fourth part of the FLIP Formula. This final step will help you focus on the value and the need for the conscious application of strategic moments of gratitude throughout your day.

I believe that gratitude fuels positive action, fuels success, and ultimately fuels *you* if you will let it. When you FLIP The Gratitude Switch and feel that shift inside, your body reacts to your choice to infuse active gratitude into your day, and that sensation will act as fuel to carry you through until the next frustration in life shows up and you can FLIP all over again.

That feeling you get from gratitude that fuels your life, and carries you is something I call powering up with #Gratifuel!

Chapter 4

P = Power-up with #Gratifuel

According to the thrilling time travel documentary better known as *Back to the Future Part II*, by the year 2015, we were all supposed to be able to fuel our vehicles' flux capacitors with banana peels and empty milk jugs. Well, apparently writer/director Robert Zemekis gave science a little too much credit, because we are still stuck using fossil fuels for now.

But what if your vehicle *could* be fueled by trash? As long as trash makes the car go vroom, that's fuel, right? No matter what fuel your car uses (fossil fuels, electricity, trash, etc.) without that fuel; it's just a useless hunk of metal.

Let's say you owned one of the most expensive cars in the world, the Lamborghini Veneno. Priced at a mere $4.5 million dollars, this impressive machine can go from zero to 60 in under three seconds, with a 750 horse-power V12 engine and a top speed of 220 mph. It basically looks like a space-ship and a Formula 1 car got married and had a car baby.

Picture yourself sitting in your new car with the anticipation of hearing the deafening roar of the engine and feeling the breathtaking accelera-tion. You are comfortably seated in the custom leather seats, surrounded by carbon fiber, and ready to see what she's got. You hit the ignition button, and … nothing. How disappointed would you feel? You just paid $4.5 million for a car that won't go one mile an hour, let alone go zero to 60 in 2.7 seconds.

All of that money and all of the incredible craftsmanship is pointless if you don't have a few bucks worth of gas to pour in the tank.

This is also true of our bodies. The human body is a finely tuned machine that heals itself and tells its owner when it needs more fuel. Our bodies know how to take in that fuel, and digest it, metabolize it, and convert it into useable energy. But what happens if you don't give your body fuel? It would begin to shut down and only function for so long before it decided it no longer could.

What about another impressive piece of equipment known as the smart phone? I often marvel at my iPhone's capabilities. My phone is my photo library and my digital camera. It's my video recorder and personal movie-editing studio. It's my movie theater, giving me access to virtually every film ever made. It's my music library. I use it as a yoga instructor, a personal trainer, and my own personal meditation guru. It's my library of books and an unlimited source of motivation thanks to the resources I can access with it. It tells the time. It tracks my meals, calorie consumption, and calories burned. It connects me globally with friends and family, enabling me to talk face to face with my parents in California, my friends in Germany, my clients in New York, and my mentors in Las Vegas, San Diego, Austin, and West Palm Beach. It is my personal navigator and can tell me, turn by turn, how to go virtually anywhere. I can book travel and use it as my boarding pass. It can be my wallet and pay for things at stores. It can be my source of religious texts and scriptures. It can act as an outlet to medical and law enforcement personnel. Oh yeah, it also can call people.

That is only a handful of the things it does. And yet, what happens if I let its little lithium battery drain down to zero? By letting the battery drain to zero, I lose access to all of those tremendous capabilities.

As much as our phones can do, their potential pales in comparison to the potential *we* have to impact the world. We have each been divinely created for a specific purpose that is far bigger, and has a far broader ripple effect than we could ever understand.

However, if we allow our life batteries to drain down, if we run out of fuel for life, we lose our potential to create that change in the world that only we can bring to pass. We need fuel for our vehicles and we need fuel for our bodies, but what about this thing we call life? What can we use as life fuel?

It's simple. We can use gratitude, because *gratitude fuels life!*

Fuel for the Soul

The FLIP Formula and the process of FLIPping the Gratitude Switch can create and deliver unlimited amounts of the fuel that will enable us to keep going and making a difference in our own lives and in the lives of others.

We can 1) Find the frustration, 2) Look for what's awesome, and 3) Initiate and feel gratitude, and when we do those things, it creates an explosion of joy that propels us forward. That combination of actions helps us keep going, knowing that we always have a way to navigate the tumultuous waters of life, and knowing that we have a constant source of fuel to keep us going through all of it.

That is why the final step of the FLIP Formula is to "Power-up With #gratifuel."

As I began sharing my experiences with gratitude, I noticed I kept using the phrase, "Gratitude fuels life." A good friend of mine named Gary Norris loved the phrase and decided to make a hybrid word out of it. He said to me one day, "Hey Kev, why don't you just say *Gratifuel?*"

Of course, I did—and it has become a huge part of this gratitude movement. Gary gave me a new word to describe something that I had found to be absolutely true:

Gratitude is the power source for life's batteries.

We each have something massive to accomplish in this life, but how often do each of us get weighted down, stressed, and overwhelmed by life? If you are like me before I discovered #Gratifuel, then your answer might be, "All the time!"

Since I've found the simple power that lies in the daily, conscious application of gratitude during times of struggle and stress, I now feel that my life batteries are always full. I am significantly less stressed; I have more energy; I have a desire to eat better and cleaner foods; I have less of a desire to be right in a business meeting.

All in all, I'm a changed man because I power up with #Gratifuel every single day. All it takes is at least one conscious decision to experience gratitude and BOOM—my day changes its entire course, making it even easier to choose gratitude the next time something frustrating happens.

Powering up with #Gratifuel is essential to the success, happiness, and ease of my day. As I mentioned in the previous chapter, I try to FLIP the Gratitude Switch as early as possible upon waking. I know that I will be in the bathroom first thing in the morning, which is why I installed my first "FLIP THE GRATITUDE SWITCH" light switch cover there.

I can't tell you how many times that visual reminder has saved my day. One morning, for example, I awoke at 4:00am and went into the kitchen to grab a bottle of water. We were out of bottled water, and I started to grumble about forgetting to pick some up at the store the night before.

I sensed my discontent, and as I went in the bathroom and physically FLIPped the Gratitude Switch on my wall, I also FLIPped my internal Gratitude Switch by applying all four parts of the FLIP Formula. I immediately thought about how lucky I was to have unlimited access to clean tap water, and I said to myself, "There are many people in the world who are not so lucky."

I let that feeling power me up with an energy of joy—and because of that moment, I had already given myself my first dose of #Gratifuel for the day. The Gratitude Switch had been flipped, and I immediately felt my life batteries fill up with #Gratifuel.

I was on my way to a fantastic day.

It is important that you complete the FLIP Formula in its entirety by noticing how you are able to power up with #Gratifuel as you go through the process. Just as part one of the FLIP Formula requires you to become conscious to your frustrations, powering up with #Gratifuel also requires you to become present and acknowledge how different you feel inside once you initiate gratitude.

The feeling is like what I imagine Mario feels when he finds a mushroom in Super Mario Brothers. It fills you up in such an amazing way, and when you become aware that you feel different inside, it will breed even more gratitude in that very moment. When you breed more gratitude by acknowledging the feeling of soulful gratitude, that feeling powers up your life batteries even more.

It's the *exact opposite* of a vicious cycle—it's actually what Dr. Alex Korb calls a "virtuous cycle." This #Gratifuel cycle is like putting enough gas in the tank to get you to the next gas station of life where you can either put in a little more #Gratifuel, or even fill it up all the way.

Drinking Your Daily Dose of #Gratifuel

There are so many things to remember in our daily lives, from setting the garbage cans out and turning off the stove, to taking the kids to soccer and the important meeting with a new client, to everything in between.

That's why I'm a fan of anything that makes the task of remembering easier. In addition to having physical Gratitude Switches in my life to help remind me to FLIP the Gratitude Switch often and consistently, I have discovered another trick to help me remember to fuel of with #Gratifuel on a regular basis.

It's really simple—here's what you do:

First, purchase a nice, clear water bottle. Then take a permanent marker and write #Gratifuel on the side. Every time you take a drink from that bottle, I want you to visualize gratitude being taken in through your mouth, down your throat, and then spreading throughout your body. Picture it being converted into the fuel you need to get through the next few minutes or hour of your day.

Whenever you pick up this water bottle, set an intention in your mind that as soon as you take a sip, you will immediately feel a greater sense of gratitude wash through your body.

Keep this water bottle with you always. Drink from it often, each time telling yourself that you are consuming pure #Gratifuel!

The Science of Gratitude

You may be wondering why you feel different inside after you feel and express gratitude. Would it surprise you if I told you the reason you feel so energized and amazing after you FLIP the Gratitude Switch is because your body has been hardwired to get a reward every time you do?

Scientifically speaking, when you experience gratitude, your body releases a chemical called *dopamine*. In a brain that is full of chemicals, dopamine seems to be the one that everyone is most familiar with. If there were a celebrity among brain chemicals, then it would be dopamine. In fact, neuroscientist Vaughan Bell once called dopamine the "Kim Kardashian of neurotransmitters" (sorry dopamine, I know that was harsh).

According to author Simon Sinek, dopamine is one of the "happiness chemicals" that our body produces and releases. Dopamine is also referred to as the *reward chemical* or the *goal-achieving chemical*. It is also addictive, which can make it dangerous. In his book, *Leaders Eat Last,* Sinek says it is only dangerous when it is abused.

Cocaine, alcohol, and nicotine are prime examples of things that send dopamine rushing through our bodies. When our bodies release dopamine, it gives us an instant gratification-type feeling and creates a pleasure sensation.

Addictive substances aren't the only things that surge dopamine through your system. Feats like accomplishing tasks and reaching big goals will also give you that dopamine release. That is why you feel so awesome when you get something accomplished that was really difficult. It also works when you accomplish something small, like checking an item off your to-do list.

I even feel this happen when I go grocery shopping. My wife and I make our grocery list on an iPhone app. As I wander around the store collecting all the odds and ends on the list, my app lets me check a box that removes collected items so I can only see the remaining items on the list. When I finish the list, the app triggers a cartoon animation and confetti blows all over my screen. It makes me feel awesome, like I accomplished something.

If something that insignificant can release dopamine, think of how powerfully dopamine can be triggered when you can FLIP frustration into gratitude.

Here is another way you may have noticed the dopamine release without realizing it. Have you ever woken up in the morning and checked your phone right away to see if you got an email, a text, or a reply to your Facebook post that you were expecting from the night before? That compelling urge is you wanting a little hit of dopamine, and the buzz, alert, or ring tone you hear gives it to you.

Ever wonder why teenagers are constantly staring at their phones? SnapChat might as well be called the Dopamine Factory, which would explain why my sixteen-year-old niece spends hours taking random selfies of portions of her face, hoping to get similar Snaps in return.

We frankly aren't any better as adults. Have you ever been sitting in a meeting, talking to your spouse, or playing with your kids when your phone beeps, and you feel compelled to rudely ignore the actual human beings in front of you so you can reply to the text? That is because not only is dopamine a reward chemical, but that reward you get also triggers a desire to take action. The text comes in, you get your hit of dopamine, you feel amazing, and then you feel compelled to respond to the text right away.

Dopamine is fueling that entire process.

Dopamine doesn't exactly require you to think rationally, which explains why as a parent, even though I worry about how quickly my kids are growing up, I still engage in texting or reading Facebook updates, turning my attention away from the little humans doing something cute right in front of me. If I were thinking rationally (made difficult by the dopamine surges we chase), I would not even touch my phone so I could savor each moment I get with my children.

Need more proof that dopamine may cause us to act irrationally? Have you ever wondered why people feel the need to respond to a text even though they are going 70 mph on the freeway? Dopamine. You feel incomplete if you don't respond right away, and that nagging feeling creates a black hole in your soul that just has to be filled immediately. Thanks a lot, dopamine.

The next time your spouse gets mad at you for checking your Facebook feed or responding to a text in the middle of the deep conversation you are supposed to be having, just blame the dopamine. See how that works for you... especially you men.

You are hardwired to feel awesome when you express gratitude, and the reason is because gratitude is one of the best ways to get that next hit of dopamine. The good news is that as soon as you FLIP the Gratitude Switch and fuel up with #Gratifuel, your body powers up with dopamine, and you will feel a compulsion to keep going. You will be fueled to keep feeling gratitude because of the sensation it gives you.

Wouldn't it be great to get addicted to the dopamine hits you get from gratitude rather than being addicted to the ones you get from social media and text messages?

Gratitude serves as a positive way to get your dopamine fix, and those hits of dopamine, as long as they are obtained in ways that help you rather than harm you, have a lot of additional benefits to you.

There is a lot more scientific research available on the positive effects of gratitude than I ever imagined when I first started researching the subject. While you may not see it often in the media, about once or twice a year (usually around Thanksgiving), a large news source will feature an article about the effects that gratitude can have on you.

If you really dig deeply, however, there are piles of data on the subject. Unfortunately, most of it goes unpublicized for the sake of more "pressing" matters like what Angelina wore to the Oscars or some propaganda news piece meant to scare us or make us buy something we don't need.

But the research is out there — and one of the best articles I read about the neuroscience of giving thanks is an article published in *Psychology Today* written by Alex Korb, Ph.D, called "The Grateful Brain." Here is an excerpt from the article:

"...improvements in gratitude [can] have such wide-ranging effects [as] increased exercise, and improved sleep to decreased depression and fewer aches and pains.

"Furthermore, feelings of gratitude directly activate brain regions associated with the neurotransmitter dopamine. Dopamine feels good to get, which is why it's generally considered the 'reward' neurotransmitter. But dopamine is also almost important in initiating action. That means increases in dopamine make you more likely to do the thing you just did. It's the brain saying, 'Oh, do that again.'

"Gratitude can have such a powerful impact on your life because it engages your brain in a virtuous cycle. Your brain only has so much power to focus its attention. It cannot easily focus on both positive and negative stimuli.

"So once you start seeing things to be grateful for, your brain starts looking for more things to be grateful for. That's how the virtuous cycle

108

gets created."

Dr. Korb also states that, "Gratitude takes practice like any other skill." The good news for you and me is that we know exactly how to exercise our gratitude muscles and practice gratitude by making it actionable through the FLIP Formula.

Fuel for Life

Life is this constant gift that takes place every second of every day, and as it's happening, it often feels like we are not the ones controlling it. It may feel like we are constantly reacting to life as it happens. We may feel like life constantly surprises us, so how could we possibly be prepared for it?

This is why I love gratitude.

When we live with gratitude in our hearts, we don't have to be constantly bracing for what may come our way, because we always have the best and most effective tool to deal with life regardless of what it throws at us.

Having the knowledge of the Gratitude Switch and how simple it is to FLIP, and understanding the importance of the conscious, daily act of FLIPping that switch will equip you with the ability to thrive in any environment and in any situation.

As you drink from your #Gratifuel water bottle throughout the day, feel yourself charging your life battery with life sustaining gratitude. You will never feel as though your life tank is on empty. You will never have to experience the drain of life's batteries if you are willing to fuel up with gratitude every day.

You will be filled up with #Gratifuel, and you will feel it physically fuel you on to the next challenge or frustration in life. When you fill up regularly with #Gratifuel, your life battery may experience a temporary drain, but the instant you FLIP the Gratitude Switch, you become like a video game character who just found some magical "power up" potion. (Of course, in our case, the magic potion is our reward and action chemical called dopamine.)

When you make FLIPping the Gratitude Switch a regular occurrence, the FLIP Formula will become a part of you. Even better, after daily deliberate use, FLIPping will deposit gratitude into your soul, and it will give you a fresh and constant supply of fuel for your life.

FLIP Formula Cheat Sheet

It is the simple, daily, consistent, conscious decision to enact gratitude at key strategic moments throughout the day by FLIPping The Gratitude Switch through the four-part FLIP Formula that is the single largest driver of success, and the single most important factor to your ongoing happiness and complete fulfillment in life.

Here is a brief instruction guide on how to turn gratitude into a verb and FLIP The Gratitude Switch:

Find The Frustration
Look For What's Awesome
Initiate Gratitude
Power-up With #Gratifuel

F stands for "Find the frustration." This is the common, frequent act of reacting to and recognizing frustrations as they arise throughout the course of your day. When something happens that is the least bit frustrating, acknowledge it, and realize you are being given the gift of initiating the FLIP Formula.

L stands for "Look for what's awesome." Now that you've located the frustration, isolate that frustration in the moment and analyze it for something that can be considered awesome. Find the blessing embedded in the hardship, the joy embedded in despair, and the success embedded in the failure.

I stands for "Initiate gratitude." Now that you have located and isolated the frustration, and found the blessing embedded in the hardship, you now get to choose to *experience* gratitude for that blessing you've located. This is the moment that the Gratitude Switch is flipped, and the moment everything changes by truly activating the power of gratitude. Face the frustration and say, "Thank you for being my teacher."

P stands for "Power up with #Gratifuel." Now that you have experienced and activated gratitude, allow the internal feeling you're experiencing to fuel you onto the next frustration or hardship you may encounter, and then repeat the four-part FLIP Formula and FLIP the Gratitude Switch again, and again, and again.

PART IV

The Life of a FLIPer

Chapter 1

To FLIP or Not to FLIP

Throughout this book, I've said over and over again that a single, small decision to FLIP the Gratitude Switch at strategic moments in your day can change the trajectory of your day, your, week, and your life. Now that you've read about the FLIP Formula, I'd like to demonstrate exactly what I mean by that.

So, let's use our imaginations for a moment. Picture yourself as the manager of the footwear department at a chain sporting goods store. You are successful, your numbers are fantastic, and you've developed really good relationships with both your customers and your employees. You think you might be up for a promotion (at least you hope so). You also have a family who loves you.

All in all, life is pretty good.

One morning, you are walking out of the kitchen with your favorite green smoothie in hand, and your four-year-old comes bounding down and wraps herself around your legs. She hits you with all the velocity, excitement, and love she possesses—and your green smoothie spills all over your clothes.

Welcome to the moment of decision.

You can decide to apply the FLIP Formula and FLIP the Gratitude Switch.

Or you can choose <u>not</u> to FLIP the Gratitude Switch.

Life Without FLIPping

In this instance, you choose not to FLIP the Gratitude Switch—and you immediately fill with anger and frustration. "Brylee, you need to be more careful! Look before you come running over to hug me. I had a smoothie in my hand. GEEZ!"

You begin loudly grumbling as you make your way back to the kitchen. "Oh great, now I have to change clothes, which means I'm definitely going to be late. The Store Manager is going to be furious, and I just know she's going to chew me out... GREAT! So much for all the hard work I've put in lately... all thrown out the window because of this stupid green smoothie and because my daughter can't look where she's going."

As you start peeling off your wet, sticky, green shirt, you turn to your daughter. "You know, Brylee, I really wish you hadn't done that. I've been trying not to be late a single day this year so I can start making more money. I haven't been late one time in four months and now, because you weren't careful, I'm going to break my streak. Daddy's big boss from corporate is flying in today to meet Daddy, and maybe give me a promotion, which means Daddy would make more money. Now, if I don't get this promotion because I'm late, we aren't going to have the money to go to Disneyland for your birthday. So, if we don't go, you will know why. Maybe next time you'll be more careful!"

You dismiss your child, who is now crying because she made you mad, and you stomp into your closet to change your clothes, muttering under your breath about how displeased you are with the whole situation.

You finally get changed and fly out the door. You furiously open your car door and sit down, turn on the engine and rip out of the driveway, squealing your tires just to make certain that everyone knows you are not happy.

Worried you are going to be late; you start speeding down the road and roll right through a stop sign, too blinded by fury to notice. A minute later, you gaze into your rearview and realize that siren you've been hearing is intended for you.

The officer gives you a ticket. He might have let you off with a warning, but considering how rude you were to him, he decides to write a ticket for the maximum fine.

Now you are really seething with anger.

You arrive at the store a half hour late, and as soon as you make your way onto the floor, you notice that one of your employees did not properly display the new running shoe that just arrived. The corporate big wig is flying in today, and the floor needs to look perfect. You reprimand the employee so severely that she quits on the spot.

You have eclipsed anger. You are practically foaming at the mouth.

Just then, your boss approaches you from behind and says your name. You have been annoyed at her micromanagement style lately, and thanks to the morning you've had so far, your aggravation with her culminates the moment she makes the first peep. She begins, "Hey, I want to introduce—"

You cut her off as you snap around, "Yes, your majesty, what is it *NOW?!*" A look of shock and dismay washes over her face as she introduces you to the corporate executive by her side.

Your boss continues, "Mr. Thompson flew here to meet you to discuss a possible promotion to manage your own store."

Jaw dropped, you stutter, "W… w… we… well, uh, thanks for the consideration. Um, can I uh, answer any questions for you?"

The executive looks at you wryly and says with suspicion, "Pleasure to meet you?"

You are mortified. "Yes sir, I'm sorry for my brisk tone. It's been a

116

tough day."

Mr. Thompson looks you in the eye. "Actually, I don't think we need to do an interview after all. I've seen everything I need to see."

Your heart sinks as you realize you have just blown your shot at a major promotion and pay raise. After a tortuous eight-hour day—where you had to do double the work on account of your employee quitting—you drive home feeling dejected, exhausted, and disappointed.

You pull in the driveway and walk into the front door, thinking how happy you are that your little one will soon be bouncing up to come give you a hug, this time with no green smoothie in sight. You could really use a hug.

Instead of seeing your little girl bounding down the hall as usual, your spouse appears with a sour look on her face. "What happened this morning?"

"What do you mean?" Does your spouse know about the disaster at the store? Is she mad about the stained shirt you left on the kitchen counter? What could it be?

If only those were the reasons. Instead, your spouse informs you, "As soon as Brylee heard your car, she ran in her room and hid. I asked her what was wrong, and she started sobbing. She kept saying, 'Did Daddy get in trouble so now we can't go to Disneyland?' I have no idea what she is talking about, but she won't come out of her room. Hearing your car pull in the driveway is usually the highlight of her day. What happened?"

You realize your overreaction to an innocent accident has not only caused you to get a ticket, lose an employee, offend your boss, and miss the promotion you've been waiting for, but it also caused your daughter to feel responsible for something painful.

What if, for the rest of her childhood, your little girl hesitates every time she considers giving you a hug? It may not seem like much, but if she senses that running up and hugging you caused you to be angry and triggered a series of bad things, there is no way to know how long that feeling could last.

When we choose to interact with life in a way that causes us to feel anger and frustration, we usually take out that frustration on those around us. We rarely consider the impact we have on other people, and what we may trigger in the world around us because of our bad mood.

And here's the thing—your *sphere of influence* (what other lives your life touches) is far bigger than you realize. Let's examine that idea using our fictional story…

Remember how you were rude to the police officer? He was just trying to do his job as he was hand delivered more proof that "people in this town simply do not respect authority." What if that frustration causes him to be a little too rough with someone else later that day? All of a sudden, his life and his job could be in jeopardy because he reacted extremely. This reaction gets caught on camera and posted on YouTube—and you triggered it all.

What if the employee who quit can't find a new job? She is a single mother, and now she has a hard time feeding her little ones. She begins to

117

feel such stress and anxiety that her loving demeanor turns to an angry one, and she starts snapping at her children, causing untold amounts of emotional scarring.

What if your boss views you differently and begins making plans to make a change to your position or eliminate your position altogether? What if she starts to treat other managers the way you treated her, and they in turn begin to treat their staff with disrespect? The store may suffer and see a decline in revenue as a ripple effect of the new management style. And now her position, your position, and the store itself may all be in jeopardy because of you.

What if the executive returns to the corporate office and the Board of Directors thinks he is incompetent because he spent all of that money to go interview a bad apple? They view him as irresponsible and begin to change some of the duties they give him, thus beginning a quiet, prolonged, and painful exit for him.

I understand that every person in this fictional story has the ability and the choice to FLIP their own Gratitude Switches after they interact with you, but you can't count on that. Once you know how to FLIP the switch, it becomes your responsibility not only to live these principles, but also to share them with others through your words, and most importantly, through your example.

What Happens If You DO Power-up with #Gratifuel?

The fictional version of you made a choice not to FLIP. But what if you had made a different choice? What if you had chosen to FLIP the Gratitude Switch? We are going to back it up to the morning of the *green smoothie spill heard around the world:*

…one morning, you are walking out of the kitchen with your favorite green smoothie in hand, and your four-year-old comes bounding down and wraps herself around your legs. She hits you with all the velocity, excitement, and love she possesses — and your green smoothie spills all over your clothes.

Welcome to the moment of decision.

In your frustration, you quickly run through the four-part FLIP Formula in your head. You immediately find the frustration, isolate and acknowledge it, and then look for and locate what is awesome in that frustration. You think about how lucky you are. "What a blessing that this little angel loves me so much that she would run that fast and hug me that hard!"

You immediately initiate and feel gratitude for the love of your daughter, and you express it by saying, "Brylee, you are one fast runner. That was about the best hug ever. Thank you!" You immediately feel the sense of gratitude in your bones, and it gives you this surge of joy and energy. You feel your life batteries fill up with some #gratifuel, and you view the moment as an opportunity to make your little girl laugh.

You start licking your shirt saying, "MMMMMMM shirt smoothie, that's my favorite kind of smoothie. Hey Brylee, you want some?" You pretend to chase her and she giggles and thinks, "My Dad is the BEST!"

You gently remind her to try to be careful, but you say with a wink and a smile, "Hey Brylee, thanks for that. I wasn't really in love with this outfit, anyway. Do you want to come help Daddy pick out a new one?"

Brylee takes joy in helping you pick out your new outfit, and once she picks out the tackiest shirt you own, you throw it on and say, "There we go—much better! Thank you sweetheart!" You watch your little girl blush with pride that she helped you.

You drive to work like a normal human and not a maniac, avoiding the ticket and arriving just a few minutes late. No one even noticed.

You don't snap at your employee, you don't greet your boss with that angry tone, and when you meet the executive, he smiles, points to your ear, and asks you, "Do you know you have something green on your ear?" Embarrassed, you wipe it off as you relate the funny experience with your daughter.

He smiles. "I appreciate a family man; I have a little girl myself. Kids are the best. Listen, I would like to take you to lunch and talk about your future with our company."

With the simple FLIP of the Gratitude Switch, done the very instant life came hurling at you, and at that exact moment of choice, you manage to avoid scarring your daughter, getting a ticket, losing an employee and a promotion, and that tiny decision to apply all four parts of the FLIP Formula was the decision that launched the success of your future, thus changing the entire trajectory of your life.

That is what is so powerful about this simple idea of FLIPping the Gratitude Switch and powering up your life with #Gratifuel.

The Best Results Require Practice

One of the best ways to begin implementing and actively FLIPping the Gratitude Switch and powering up with #Gratifuel on a regular basis is to discuss these principles with other people in your life. You are now part of an elite group of individuals who know that the key to happiness and success is in your possession, and it is as simple as flipping a switch. There are so many people you love and respect in your life that need to hear this message!

Head over to the book website, **FLIPTheGraitutdeSwitch.com**, or go to Amazon and consider buying another copy so that you can gift it to someone in your life. The two of you can become part of this movement together and help each other charge your life batteries daily with #Gratifuel.

If you can't afford another book, begin using the principles, and you will be able to afford another book in no time. Worst case scenario—loan them this copy, and allow this book to begin opening up powerful conversations with those you love most in your life.

Life is going to keep happening whether you ask it to or not, so how do you fuel your life to carry you from whatever point you find yourself this moment, to the point you want to arrive at one day? Are you properly equipped to handle all it's going to hurl at you?

Cars have gasoline, and smart phones have lithium batteries. What do you have?

You have #gratifuel!

One FLIP can fill up your life battery until the next opportunity to use the FLIP Formula, or it could even fuel you for the entire day. Gratitude will always fuel you from point A to point B, but when used consistently, it will fuel your entire life.

Consistency is the key. Over time, as you begin to see how simple it is to apply the FLIP Formula during every single frustrating moment throughout the day, the FLIP Formula and the act of FLIPping The Gratitude Switch will become a part of the fiber of your being.

You will be a walking vessel of gratitude, and whatever life throws at you, you will have the exact process you need to both deal with life and *thrive* as a result of it.

Are you still wondering whether one tiny FLIP could have an impact on your life and on your happiness levels? It's completely natural to question what we see and hear. In fact, we should do it more often!

The next chapter will reveal the results of the "gratitude experiment" I conducted to prove whether FLIPping the Gratitude Switch could really increase your happiness levels and containment with your life. (Spoiler alert: IT REALLY WORKS!)

Chapter 2

Let's get Sciency

Remember the Harris Poll that reported two-thirds of us consider ourselves to be unhappy? When I undertook the task of writing this book, I knew I needed to present something that legitimized my beliefs about the power of gratitude and proved that gratitude could move the barometer on those two-thirds of us that the Poll measured as "unhappy." I thought, wouldn't it be great to find a way to measure someone's current happiness (or unhappiness) level at any given moment? And it would be even better if I could measure a happiness increase over time as a result of consistently FLIPping the Gratitude Switch. I thought if I could do that, then I could share with you some scientific data that proves everything we have talked about in this book so far to be absolutely real and true.

This chapter is for the small percentage of you that have read this book up to this point and are still thinking, "This all sounds good in theory, but is this actually something real?" Here is your proof!

Putting on My Scientist Hat

I sought after volunteers to participate in a four-week happiness experiment that included applying gratitude in their daily lives, keeping track of their experiences, and taking a weekly quiz.

I wanted to see if the consistent use of conscious gratitude could increase levels of contentment, life satisfaction, and overall happiness. I obviously believe it can do all of that and more, but if I could measure it, then it would allow others (maybe even you) to take this formula for happiness more seriously.

I purposely did not overwhelm the volunteers with the details regarding the FLIP Formula, and I also left the phrase "FLIP the Gratitude Switch" out of the quizzes and instructions. I knew if I taught them about the principles before I started testing, the participants might give me the responses they thought I wanted. I needed them to remain as unbiased as possible. I simply instructed them to apply small amounts of gratitude during moments of frustration, write down a few of their experiences, and take a weekly quiz.

Nearly 100 people agreed to be a part of my little experiment. I knew this was a relatively small sample size, but I also thought that the number would be easy to manage and measure.

Now, I'm not exactly the most Sciency (that's a word, right?) guy out there, but this stuff is necessary to validate the ideas in this book. If you dislike quantitative studies, just skip ahead to the section titled, "The Results Are In." For those of you who love numbers, analytics, and statistics — let's get sciency!

The Happiness Quiz

The volunteers began their journey by taking a quiz. It was the same quiz they would be taking each week for the entire duration of the experiment. I started with the quiz because I needed a baseline from which to measure the decrease or increase in their happiness levels as the weeks progressed. I wanted to measure how happy they felt about things and life in general *before* they learned about and applied gratitude.

Then I asked participants, at least once a day, to make a conscious decision to feel and experience gratitude when a frustration arose. I instructed them, "If you feel yourself getting frustrated, angry, hurt, annoyed, etc, simply find the silver lining or what's awesome embedded in the minor frustration, the anger, or the hurt, and focus on being thankful, just for a moment, for the silver lining within that frustration."

I asked them to write down at least one sentence at least once a day about the experience of consciously choosing gratitude during the moments of frustration.

Once a week, I asked them to log in on their own time to take the same quiz they had taken at the beginning so I could compare answers and track progression. I felt that if I were breathing down their necks, they could feel resentment when taking the weekly quiz, which would have a negative impact on the quiz results (or at least cause the data to become skewed). By letting them take the quiz at their own pace, and according to their own schedule, I reasoned their results would contain more purity of measurement.

The weekly quiz consisted of forty-questions that included 25 positive and 15 negative statements that each required a response. Negative statements were things like, "I feel that I am not especially in control of my life." An example of a positive statement was, "I find it easy to smile." The statements were presented in random order each time so the participants didn't sense a pattern of positive and negative trends.

The participants were asked to respond to each statement using a six-option spectrum that ranged from "strongly disagree" to "strongly agree." If a person answered "strongly agree" in response to "I find it easy to smile," it indicated that individual had a higher level of happiness than someone who answered, "strongly disagree" to the same prompt.

Conversely, a response of "strongly disagree" to the prompt, "I feel that I am not especially in control of my life," told me this person felt he/she was in control of his/her life. I obviously would record such a response as positive, indicating that this person likely possesses more happiness than someone who answered, "strongly agree" to the prompt, "I feel that I am not especially in control of my life."

How Did I Get The Scores?

I wanted to see if I could mathematically prove that for a small sample group, the daily application of the FLIP Formula — even with the test takers not fully understanding the information contained in this book — could in fact, on paper, prove that the application of gratitude improves happiness levels.

Of those of who initially agreed to take the quiz, roughly 20 percent did not participate once the experiment was underway. In other words, I never received a single quiz result from them. Another 20 percent only took one quiz. I threw out their responses because I had no way to measure an increase or decrease in the level of happiness through their application and activation of daily gratitude.

Of the remaining participants, 56 percent took two quizzes, 19 percent took three quizzes, and 25 percent of the participants took at least four quizzes over four consecutive weeks.

In order to quantitatively measure results, I turned the six possible responses into numerical values so that I could actually measure potential increases in life contentment and happiness as a direct result of the daily application of gratitude I was asking them to implement. Here is how the points system looked:

Strongly disagree	= 1
Moderately disagree	= 2
Slightly disagree	= 3
Slightly agree	= 4
Moderately agree	= 5
Strongly agree	= 6

After I compiled all of the quiz results, I took the 40 questions and divided them into negative statements and positive statements. I knew I would have to measure the responses to the negative and positive statements separately because I would have a different desired outcome for each of the sets of statements. In other words:

- I hoped the POSITIVE statements' responses would INCREASE in the average score over the time frame of the experiment.
- I hoped the NEGATIVE statements' responses would DECREASE in numerical value as the experiment went along.

If the numerical values that correlated to the responses decreased among the negative statements and increased among the positive statements, I would consider that statistical proof of gratitude improving the lives of my small sample group.

To explain this further, let's take a look at a negative statement. At the beginning of week one before the application of gratitude began, if the respondent answered the prompt "I feel that I am not especially in control of my life," with "slightly agree," it indicated that this person felt a little bit like he/she does not have much control over life. I gave this a numerical value of 4.

In week two of the experiment—after participants had started tracking their gratitude experiences daily and FLIPping the Gratitude Switch daily—if the same individual responded to the same statement with "slightly disagree," that person moved from a 4 to a 3. For the negative statements, that would be as statistical improvement.

By the end of the experiment, if the daily, conscious application of gratitude took the respondent from an answer of "slightly agree" (or a 4) to "strongly disagree" (or a 1), it indicated that this person now feels completely in control of his/her life. What I ended up with, then, was a quantitative representation of an increase in the individual's happiness and contentment level due to FLIPping the Gratitude Switch daily.

All of the same reasoning applies to the positive statements with a few minor differences. An example of a positive statement from the quiz is, "I feel that I have a personal mission in life."

Let's say an individual taking the quiz responded with a "slightly disagree" (a value of 3) to this statement during week one. In week two, this person responded, "slightly agree" (a value of 4) to that statement. In week three, the response was "moderately agree" (a value of 5). And in the final week, he/she responded with "strongly agree" (a value of 6) to the same statement.

Such an increase over time proved to me that the theory of the daily, conscious, application of gratitude at key strategic moments throughout the day does, in fact, increase one's happiness level and overall level of contentment with their life.

Now that we understand how the quiz was structured, implemented, scored, and measured, let's take a look at the results!

The Results Are In

I imagined I would see a net increase in the happiness and contentment levels of those who participated, but there were some unexpected results that proved my theory even better than I had hoped.

With all numbers and results combined, the participants collectively saw an increase in happiness by a total of 12 percent by simply choosing to apply gratitude daily. They were 12 percent happier, on paper, than they had been four weeks earlier, according to the responses to both the negative and positive prompts and how I scored them.

This is where it gets interesting. I certainly did not expect each participant to be perfect in taking the quizzes, and certainly not in applying gratitude on a daily basis. It takes practice and a conscious application of the FLIP Formula to develop that discipline.

However, there were a few fascinating occurrences.

Everyone who volunteered started out with a desire to participate daily. Of course, there were some who only took one quiz, some who took two, a few who took three quizzes, and a group that took all four. In talking with participants, it turns out that IF they remembered to regularly FLIP the Gratitude Switch, they would also remember to take the quiz.

Here is what this means—those who only took two quizzes only did the experiment for two weeks. The same goes for those who did three quizzes and four quizzes. The more quizzes they took, the more accurately I could track their increase in happiness level because more quizzes meant they were more regularly engaging in the application of gratitude.

After I had measured the overall results, I decided to break down the happiness increase into separate two-quiz, three-quiz, and four-quiz groups. Here is what I found:

- Those who took just two quizzes saw a total of a 9 percent increase in happiness during the two weeks in which they applied gratitude to their lives.
- Those who took three quizzes saw a total of a 14 percent increase in happiness during the three weeks.
- Those who took all four quizzes saw a total of a 19 percent increase in happiness during the four-week period!

I certainly did not expect that I would be able to measure those kinds of results. In fact, when I first started to download the quiz results, I was slightly irritated. I thought that since a good number of those who agreed to take the quizzes and FLIP the Gratitude Switch daily had not done what I'd hoped for, the end result would be inaccurate results.

That minor irritation gave me an opportunity to FLIP my own Gratitude Switch—and that is a story worth telling. I was entering data and fuming a little, feeling like way too many people hadn't lived up to the commitment they made. Feeling this frustration, I knew I had to pause for a moment and consider my own FLIP Formula. Here is what it sounded like inside my head:

"I'm a little bugged more people didn't follow the instructions and do all four quizzes. Wait, that is a frustration. Oh, good! That means there is something awesome I can look for!

"I wonder if there are enough people who only took two quizzes, three quizzes, and four quizzes that I can measure their results separately? Then I can see if there was a happiness increase in the four-week quiz takers that exceeds the happiness increase of the other two groups.

"If there were, that would be awesome.

"I'm really thankful that some of the participants didn't take the quiz all four weeks. They provided me with a wider variety of data to look at and possibly even helped me paint an even richer picture. Let me take a moment and feel how lucky I am that it worked out this way.

"Now I'm excited to look at all this data! I can't wait to find out what it will reveal. Let's get to work."

I soon discovered that the groups of two-quiz, three-quiz, and four-quiz takers were pretty equal in number, which worked out perfectly. And of course, the results showed that for each additional week the quiz takers experienced regular gratitude and took the quiz, their happiness level increased by an extra 5 percent per week.

I never would have found that out or even thought to look for that correlation, without having personally FLIPped the Gratitude Switch. That one FLIP created a whole new dimension to my understanding of the reliability of the FLIP Formula.

In short, my experiment empirically proved that the daily, conscious decision to apply and use gratitude could increase your happiness and your contentment.

Hopefully at this point, you understand that we *need* gratitude, but do you fully understand why? Why is it that life can seem so complicated and hard? What are the influences that are causing us to feel that life is tougher than we imagined, or not quite the life we expected or even hoped for?

In the next chapter, I will talk about the mistake we often make by choosing to view life through lenses of limitation which can often cause our view of our reality to be clouded, and tricks our mind into thinking things are worse than they have to be, and some of the constant social influences that seem to constantly beckon and tempt us to put on our lenses of limitation.

Chapter 3

Lenses of Limitation vs. Gratitude Glasses

Imagine taking off early from work one afternoon to go see the new mega hit blockbuster movie you've been dying to see. You walk into the theater lobby and are immediately blasted with the seductive aroma of popcorn. You breathe in deeply, already savoring the next 120 minutes of freedom and escape from real life.

You walk up to the ticket counter and request a ticket with money in hand. The ticket price is higher than you expected for a matinee, but you brush it off with the thought, "Oh well, prices go up from time to time."

You walk over to the snack counter and order popcorn, soda, and a box of Junior Mints. The person working the counter says, "Do you want your Junior Mints regular or frozen?"

"Wait, you have frozen ones? Awesome! I want those."

The nice young man happily hands you your goodies and takes your money, and you are off to the dark, cozy theater for some good, clean fun.

You settle into your reclining movie seat for what is sure to be an epic movie experience. The trailers finish, and the movie begins—but the opening credits seem a little blurry. You assume this is due to a directorial font choice as you continue to shovel in the popcorn, sip your soda, pop a Junior Mint or two, and wait for the big action sequence at the beginning of the movie.

The action sequence begins, but the screen still seems blurry. You rub your eyes and look around to see if anyone else seems to be having the same blurred movie viewing experience you are, and wouldn't you know it—you are all by yourself. That *never* happens!

You keep eating, drinking, and watching, hoping that the blur is just another directorial choice, or that it'll clear itself up in another minute or so. It doesn't. Every now and then, it seems like the characters pop into focus, but a moment later, the screen becomes blurry again.

You are naturally a little frustrated. You used up a half of a vacation day for this, the ticket was more expensive than you had expected, and now you are sitting here hoping for an epic movie experience, but getting only a mediocre one.

As you finish the disappointing movie experience and make your way out of the theater, you pass a theater employee who says, "Please make sure you deposit your 3D glasses in the receptacle just outside the door."

"WHAT? This movie was 3D?!"

What's the point of this little story? Well, if you were to watch a 3D movie without glasses, you would probably still understand the movie. You'd be able to follow the plot lines, enjoy the dialog, and get through it just fine. You may even have a decent time—but ask yourself, how much more enjoyable would that film have been if you realized the movie was 3D and you had grabbed some 3D glasses on your way in?

Wouldn't the movie be better? Wouldn't the visuals come to life? Wouldn't the entire experience be more dynamic, exciting, enjoyable, and vivid? You would've had a completely different experience simply by looking at the same movie through a different set of lenses.

This is a metaphor for the way many of us view life. Rather than experience life in its full potential, we view life through the *Lenses of Limitation.*

The movie that is your life can absolutely be experienced in a different way than most of us currently experiencing it. It can be more vivid, more entertaining, and significantly more enjoyable. The exact same movie you are living right now can be experienced in a different way if you so choose.

You just need the right glasses.

You need to swap out your Lenses of Limitation for a pair of Gratitude Glasses.

Most of us are sitting in the 3D movie of life with the wrong glasses on. While we are able to experience much of what it has to offer, we are missing one key component to the experience, and are therefore missing out on the full spectrum of joy, humor, love, excitement, and action that life has to offer.

Imagine a glass partially filled with water. With certain lenses on, the glass may either look half empty or half full, but I want you to consider viewing the glass differently. What if the glass isn't half empty OR half full? What if the amount of liquid in that glass, regardless of whether it is a drop or a gallon, is simply ENOUGH?

There MAY be times when the glass becomes completely drained. Even then, never should that glass be viewed as *empty*—it should only ever be viewed as re-fillable.

Gratitude Glasses allow you to view that glass and its liquid as *enough,* even plenty. Your Gratitude Glasses improve your view of the world and allow your life experiences to be filled with more happiness and satisfaction.

With Gratitude Glasses on, it is enough, because it is exactly what it is. The difference between *half empty, half full,* and *enough* is quite simply how we choose to view it.

Securely Insecure

"Everything is amazing right now and nobody's happy." That is a quote from comedian Louis CK—and boy is he right. We have all of this amazing technology at our fingertips. We can build body parts on 3D printers. We don't even think twice about astronauts going up into space anymore (that's so last century now). In a few years, we will all have cars that drive themselves. We have phones that can access any information, anytime, anywhere. And of course, we have multiple ways to instantly communicate with anyone and everyone worldwide, 24 hours a day.

Since the advent of the Internet, smart phones, and social media, there is not another time in history when communication has been so expansive. However, there has also never been more ways to compare our lives to others.

All of these technological advances and all of these new communication methods have given us more ways than ever to constantly judge whether our life is as good as the next guy or gals. We now have easier and even secretive ways to compare ourselves to and judge others, as we hide behind our social media profiles and private browsers. We "Facebook stalk" people in order to see whether we are as successful or as good as others are in virtually every aspect of our lives.

Since you are human, you will no doubt battle with some level of insecurity for the rest of your life. Insecurity seems to be fundamental to the human experience. There are all sorts of developmental reasons for how and why we create limiting beliefs, and for the stories we tell ourselves about who we are and what we deserve, but we also happen to be living in a time when technology and media have exacerbated the problem. We are constantly bombarded with reasons to slip on the Lenses of Limitation as we stare at our phone, computer, or television screens to continuously compare our lives to the lives of others.

The New Enemy of Happiness?

I love social media as much as the next person. I mean, I'm the guy who just checked Facebook, sent out a Tweet, and approved some requests on LinkedIn after checking how many YouTube views my new video got, all while posting on Instagram, and Periscoping about SnapChat. I'm serious—check out my Twitter. I bet I just posted @KevinClayson.

Despite my love of all things social media, with all its communicative and emotional benefits, I will admit that it has had, I think, another seriously unfortunate side effect. It causes many of us to think that all is well—all the time—with everyone but us. Have you ever noticed how that kind of isolation becomes a numbing agent to joy? The thought that everyone's life must be boundlessly AMAZING starts to make us question why ours isn't going nearly as well, nearly as often as everyone else's.

All of our friends seem to be on vacation, their families appear to be perfect, their jobs are the best, and everyone is living a supreme existence. We see pictures of all the awesome stuff they buy and all cool the restaurants they frequent. We learn about all the fun they are having and the concerts and sporting events they are attending. We think their marriages are perfect and their children have angel wings and flutter around playing harps and creating Go Fund Me campaigns to feed the homeless.

As a parent, chances are you've compared your kids' behavior to the other kids at school, at church, or even at the local playground. In the event your kids acted a little snotty, entitled, or bratty, you likely questioned your parenting style and doubted whether you were a good enough parent. You've scoured Facebook for some proof that your friends' children can at times be just as unruly as yours so you will feel a little better.

In your relationship, social media and modern portrayals of "love" in movies make little spats and disagreements breeding grounds for discontent. Maybe you had a little argument with your significant other and then popped in the movie, *The Notebook,* and you wondered why your love isn't like theirs. Or maybe you see a friend post something that their spouse did for them—bought flowers, cleaned the house, made dinner, achieved world peace, whatever—and you've thought, "Why can't my husband (or wife) be like *that?*"

How about weight loss? It's far too tempting to look at that Instagram post of your friend who recently gave birth and already lost her baby weight and wonder why it seems "so easy" for her to shed her baby weight when it's "just so hard" for you to get rid of these extra pounds.

And money? You may look at your neighbor's new car or boat in the driveway, or you watch a YouTube video of their recent two-month-long vacation in the Italian countryside, and think, "Geez, what are they doing to be able to afford all this stuff? And what am I doing wrong?"

After watching everyone's awesome lives unfold on a handheld high definition screen, you look in the mirror, disgusted by your appearance, depressed by your bank account, and frustrated you aren't a better parent. You may wonder why you just aren't good enough, or at a minimum, why you aren't as good as "them."

We've all been there. In fact, I would wager that most of us are there right now. It's pretty human of us to feel insecure.

We compare our lives to theirs, forgetting that *their* portrayal of *their* reality may or may not be fictitious. At worst, it may be a total fabrication. At best, their life may, in fact, be pretty awesome, but probably not THAT awesome, and certainly not THAT much more awesome than ours.

The real issue is that even if *their* lives are incredible in every way, *their* lives shouldn't affect the way we view *our lives*. Someone else's life, whether real or portrayed as real, shouldn't ever affect you as much as your own life should. In other words:

Why change your view of your own life based on what you perceive someone else's life to be like?

One of the most interesting aspects of social media is that while *their* life seems awesome to *you*, *they* may actually think that *their* life kind of stinks compared to *yours*. In fact it's pretty likely that at the same time you are comparing your life to theirs, they are comparing their life to yours (and wondering why your life is so great and theirs is not).

You really cannot judge a book by its cover, and social media only presents the "cover" of everyone's lives. We only display what we want people to see. Our posts show all the good in our lives, but most certainly not all the bad (and more than likely, NONE of the bad).

For example, we don't take a picture of the blister caused by our new shoes. Rather, we take a picture of our new shoes that *caused* the blister and say something like, "Check out my new shoes! SO cute, right? I had a super great run today breaking them in!" #ShoeFetish #LoveToShop #blessed #BeastModeRunner #FitMom #MessyHurrDontCurr

We don't take a picture of our steadily growing belly because of how much we eat out. Instead, we post a picture of our meal, conveniently forgetting to mention that it has 2700 calories. But you can be sure we *will* talk about the one thing on the plate that is gluten-free, organic, or paleo, making sure to portray just how delicious it is and how socially responsible we are for picking such a meal. We post something like, "Just tried the new, fresh, organic place downtown. Amaze fest!! The owner lived in Tibet for like 20 years... super enlightened!" #HealthyLife #organic #foodie #nomnom #EatClean

We don't take a picture that shows we can barely fit into our old gym clothes and Snap Chat it to the world. Instead, we pick the ONE selfie out of the hundred we took that makes us look skinny—and then use an Instagram filter to make us look even skinnier and probably tanner. Then we post *that* pic and check in at the gym with some kind of caption like, "Gym time!" #FitLife #GymRat #FlexFriday #workout #legendary #LegDay

Come on, you know you've done it.

We also don't take a screen shot of the negative balance in our bank account or our credit card statements totaling thousands of dollars. Instead, we take a picture of the tickets we just purchased or the plane tickets for the flight we just booked to the Caribbean next month, somehow neglecting to post that we can't afford the trip and are going into more debt to go on that vacation.

We experience a constant barrage of communication through observation from all of the people we follow, like, and are connected with through social media, and we actually begin to think that their lives are so much better than ours.

It's merely our perception, and it is the perception that is being fed to us through our Lenses of Limitation that we so willingly slip on as we open up our app or our browser.

It's certainly not reality.

Celebratizing Our Lives

Social media, celebrity gossip shows, and magazines like *US Weekly* have also made the lives of celebrities far too important to us. For some reason, we really care (and I mean, REALLY care) about every single aspect of

135

celebrities' lives. We want to know what they had for breakfast, how many times they went to the bathroom before lunch, what brand of underwear they are wearing, whether they got enough sleep last night, their thoughts on the election, their thoughts on other people's thoughts on the election... I could go on.

We have idolized them to such an extent that they are basically demigods. And thanks to this celebrity worship, we then try to "celebratize" our own lives on social media to mask the perceived monotony of our perceived boring, and non-fabulous lives.

Rapper Macklemore has a song called "Light Tunnels" that perfectly communicates what is likely the real story behind celebrities and Hollywood. In the song, Macklemore describes what it's like to be at a Hollywood red carpet awards show. He says:

> "So we Botox our skin and we smile for the camera
> Might as well get a new nose while we're at it
> This is America and insecurity's our fabric
> And we wear it and we renamed it fashion"

In the song, he also uses the phrase "insecurity dressed up as confidence," which I believe rings so true to our children today. Our children are growing up in a world where they are taught to aspire to be like these images they see on their phones, tablets, and on the big screen, images that have been touched up and no longer resemble anything that's even remotely attainable in real life. These are images of people who may end up riddled with addiction and faced with tabloid-worthy scandals. Some of the people we are being taught to worship will even lose their lives to substance abuse or suicide. These are the images our kids and we are bombarded with, and these are the images that are being dangled in front of us as the standard of "true success." They are the new heroes—and that's actually pretty terrifying.

The idea that this perceived reality is real life is the perfect example of how our kids are handed a pair of Limitation Lenses by the world around them. The infatuation we have with celebrity culture is affecting our kids as they pick up their milk in the lunch line, as they sit in class, and as they walk home from the bus stop and take in the world around them.

"Hey guilt and shame... my kids are right over here. Can you run over and make them feel bad about not being as cool, pretty, handsome, or rich as these other kids, you know, since they are so young and impressionable? Great thanks!"

Our kids need to be allowed to love and live their lives without being assaulted by a constant barrage of other people's opinions, perceptions, and standards. Our youth need to learn about how awesome this life can be, and how awesome their life *is* right now, not how it ***should*** be based on popular culture and popular trends.

As I speak to kids at middle schools and high schools as a paid speaker, and as I volunteer my speaking services to nonprofits that work with young people, I'm struck by the massive insecurity that is already setting in at such a young age in this country.

Of course, you and I were not immune to insecurity in our youth. However, as an outside observer, it does seem to be more extreme than ever before, and I believe those increased levels of insecurity have been proliferated by the portrayal of everyone else's glamorous "reality."

When I speak to these young audiences, I share stories about my life growing up. I tell them about all the times when I felt like I'd never get the girl, how I never thought I'd be cool enough, and how sometimes I used to walk down the halls and feel like no one could really see me. In relating these tales of adolescent woe, my goal is to help them realize—as I hope to help you realize—that we ALL feel this way at some point. But the media tells us we aren't "them" (celebrities, movie stars, reality stars), so we feel we have no choice but to be insecure about being us, all thanks to the perception created as we gaze through our Lenses of Limitation.

Reality TV... Anything But Reality

It is not only Social Media and our worship of movie stars and pop stars that is causing this whole "isolation that leads to loneliness with a shade of envy" way of life; there are other factors at work.

I can tell you from personal experience that there is almost nothing more damaging to your sense of self-confidence than is Reality TV. This perceived reality is nothing more than scripted tom-foolery, but it has had a profound impact on our happiness levels. We find ourselves comparing our looks and our lives to those "real" ones on the screen.

We decide we aren't as good-looking or as rich as they are, and we choose to become incensed that these "idiots" who have "zero talent" have "never worked a day in their lives," and yet now they are living a perfect existence. We see their decadent lifestyles, fame, and fortune—none of which are inherently bad, but still cause us to covet, as we wonder why a little more luck couldn't have come our way.

The real problem with Reality TV, and why I think it has led to part of the epidemic of sadness and lack of fulfillment in this world, is because we watch Reality TV and assume that it actually IS reality. We treat the "reality" presented to us on these shows in the same way we treat the "reality" presented to us on social media; the only difference is the reality shows are well funded, strategically edited, and produced by someone like Ryan Seacrest.

I have a friend who appeared on Season One of Donald Trump's reality TV show, *The Apprentice.* One of her comments during the show was used as a sound bite in a lot of the show's marketing. As she was sitting at Donald Trump's table in his Trump Tower penthouse, she said, "I wonder how many deals have been made right here at this table?!" She later told me that producers fed her that line in order to capture the exact sound bite they wanted to further their finger steepling world domination plans.

Another friend of mine was a famous villain on ABC's *The Bachelor-ette.* If you watch him on *The Bachelorette* and *Bachelor in Paradise* or watch his press (even his segment on *Dr. Phil*), he seems like the rudest, most self-centered jerk in the world. In real life, however, he is an incredibly nice and charitable individual.

What you see on TV is rarely what you get in real life.

None of this is meant as an indictment of social media, celebrities, or reality TV, I love it all; I am simply acknowledging the negative impact they can have on a world whose inhabitants lack the simple truths about FLIP-ping the Gratitude Switch. The negative impacts of social media, celebrity worship, and reality TV are merely a representation of the many ways we are unknowingly slipping on a pair of Limitation Lenses that cloud our view of real life, or rather, what life could really be. It's no wonder we feel like we lack the life we really want when we are constantly comparing ourselves to everyone and everything else.

The Nightly "Chicken Little Report"

Right about the time we start to feel really bad about our lives after a day spent reading social media feeds, watching reality TV, and reading about the latest vacation our favorite celebrity took, we turn on the nightly news.

And that's when things go from bad to worse.

I will admit that maybe I'd have a more positive opinion of the news if Ron Burgundy from the movie *Anchorman* was the one reporting it, but my reality is that the news, the evening news, newspapers, newsy blogs, and websites that report the news give humans a terrible view of this thing called life.

After a few days of reading the newspaper and watching news reports in the evening, it's easy to buy into the fallacy that all humankind is inherently bad with the exception of a few random outliers.

The nightly news programs are perhaps the worst offenders, and maybe the worst propagators of the Lenses of Limitation. They make it seem as if not a single good thing happens... EVER! The typical nightly news show might as well be called the "Chicken Little Report" because the sky is *always* falling. It seems like everyone is getting murdered, getting poisoned, getting robbed, or getting into an accident. But no worries, right! Because they will end the newscast with a little sports, a little weather, and a *riveting* story about the best place in town to go for a slice of pizza.

How are we supposed to make sense of it all? I'm not saying we ought to be naive or bury our heads in the sand. Quite the contrary! We need to become keenly aware of what is happening around us every single moment, and then we must take that reality and FLIP tough times into something incredible. We need to look at it all through our Gratitude Glasses.

The Pain Behind the Pretense

The lives that we portray to the world on the Internet and the lives we see portrayed all around us are... Just. Not. Real. Life can be hard, and guess what? It's hard for everyone else, not just you and me. People are always shocked when some story does come out about a celebrity who was secretly battling with addiction or depression. We are shocked, not because those ideas are so foreign to us, but because the life that celebrity had been *presenting* to the world didn't even hint of such struggles.

I used to constantly compare my level of success and achievement with those around me.

All of that stopped when I started FLIPping the Gratitude Switch and thereby slipping on some Gratitude Glasses.

"I don't care what your house looks like or how many square feet it has. I'm just thankful I have a roof over my head."

Switch FLIPped!

"I don't care what your body looks like. I'm just thankful I have two legs that are fully functional that I can use to go for a jog."

Switch FLIPped!

"I don't care that you have millions of dollars in your bank account. I'm just thankful I have all my needs met, I spend as much time as I want with my family, and I can give to my church AND go to Disneyworld. I feel blessed beyond measure."

Switch FLIPped!

See the idea here? You don't have to compare *you* to others... you only have to compare you to YOU! If you want to work to improve some area of your life, let it be your goal to become a better version of the person you already are, all while being THANKFUL that you are who you are this moment.

You may not have achieved the level of success you want yet, but you can be thankful for every step along the way to where you want to be. Focus on the gratitude for the tiny bit of progress made, not the deficit of desired achievement you may perceive.

I believe that most of our insecurity stems from the perception of lack, but if we become thankful for what we have, then there can be no perceived lack. If there is no of lack, then there is no reason to be insecure.

Most of the measuring sticks that we use for success, fame, and beauty are nothing more than "insecurity dressed up as confidence" anyway.

Gratitude Leads to Joy

If our lives aren't as amazing as the lives of our friends (real or cyber), if our "reality" is far from that of those people on TV and in the movies, and if the world is filled with evil like the news reports say that it is, then it is no wonder insecurity plays a role in causing our view of the world around us to become murky and convoluted.

I don't know if the FLIP Formula will heal the country or the world, but what I do know for certain is this book just handed you a simple way to instantly turn that frown upside down, as well as an invitation to slip on a pair of Gratitude Glasses. FLIPping the Gratitude Switch will make you feel better about life as it looks RIGHT NOW.

If you are part of the people out there who consider themselves happy already, then this guide to joy, and this Formula, will create even more fulfillment, contentment, and happiness than you have ever had before. I guarantee it. It reminds me of a quote by David Steindl-Rast from his book *Gratefulness, The Heart of Prayer:*

> *"It is not joy that makes us grateful.*
> *It is gratitude that makes us joyful."*

If you're guilty of posting only the good things or trying to "celebratize" your life by stretching your truths (or even fabricating some of the more dazzling details) and avoiding posting your REAL reality at all costs, that's okay! Now that you've learned how to regularly FLIP the Gratitude Switch, AND when you are authentic enough to post about the bad things that can happen, your posts will likely be followed by declarations of something good that is embedded in the bad. (I sincerely hope those posts will be followed up with a #gratifuel hashtag.)

If you still struggle with insecurities of any kind, maybe you can post something inspirational thanks to a newfound understanding of the "why" that has been fueling your insecurities. Perhaps you can share with your followers, friends, and connections how, despite your insecurities, you are pushing through and creating a new you—a fabulous and amazing version of yourself that you adore just as you are today. You can help your friends and family see that they are not alone in their insecurities, and that by FLIPping The Gratitude Switch, they can find love for themselves and their circumstances in a way that will have them looking at life through a brand new pair of Gratitude Glasses. (I also hope these posts will be followed up with a #gratifuel hashtag.)

I hope you're ready for it, but just in case you aren't, this may be a good time to pause our regularly scheduled programming for a FLIPping Public Service Announcement:

WARNING: Reading and applying this book may make you become one of those obnoxious, constantly positive, Facebook, Twitter, Instagram, and SnapChat users. Side effects may be haters hating, naysayers, poor sports, and generally dissatisfied people littering your timeline and comment threads in order to tell you how obnoxious you are and offering advice on how to reenter what they refer to as "the real world." Proceed with caution.

And now back to our regularly scheduled programming.

Those who have yet to read this book may judge you because they don't know what you know. In order to help get them up to speed, go to **FLIPTheGratitudeSwitch.com** and consider buying them a copy of the book, because it is really hard to judge someone who is being nice to you and buys you things.

If you take these principles to heart and apply them regularly, you will see your life change, and you will begin to view the world through *Gratitude Glasses* instead of the *Lenses of Limitation.*

I still deal with my own insecurities, but I no longer allow them to plague me. You *can* loosen the grip insecurities have on your life so that they no longer torment you, or perhaps more importantly, define you. If insecurities rule the roost, you are likely viewing the world through Lenses of Limitation, because you are constantly acknowledging your limiting beliefs about who you are or how worthy (more like unworthy) of love and happiness you may be.

Lenses of Limitation are the reason we feel like we are not enough. They are also what make us feel like we aren't "keeping up with the Joneses," which is why we enter into the unending, frustrating, and exhausting race to keep up, no matter the cost.

Instead of continuing to fight this perpetual and losing battle, imagine slipping on Gratitude Glasses and FLIPping the Gratitude Switch when those pesky thoughts of "I'm not enough" start to invade your head.

Do you believe you are truly blessed beyond measure?

Well, you are if you choose to be! Slip on some Gratitude Glasses and let the movie of your life slip into stunning focus, one simple FLIP of the switch at a time.

Chapter 4

The Gratitude Challenge

I sincerely hope you've enjoyed this book. I hope the FLIP Formula, and the simple ideas of *FLIP The Gratitude Switch* seem easy and clear to you.

I want you to know that for me, this book, and its message have been the fulfillment of what Napoleon Hill referred to as one's "definite major purpose." I did not know I would ever write this book; it happened organically. And once I started writing it, it transformed from what I ever even imagined it would be. In fact, if you saw my original notes and book outline, it would be almost unrecognizable. I tried to let my heart and inspiration I feel like I received from above lead me through the process of writing and assembling this book.

And I hope I have accomplished that in a way that has been beneficial for you.

I have been absolutely humbled through this experience. This message is my life's mission.

Many of us go through life not ever really knowing if we are having an impact on the world around us. We get up, go to work, pay the bills, try to relax, and try to be good people. The Daily Grind doesn't always feel conducive to fulfilling our life's mission. Well, I want you to know that by you taking just a couple minutes a day to feel gratitude, you will totally change the trajectory of your day, and ultimately the feeling that your life's mission is being fulfilled.

The fact that you have given me some of your time by reading and experiencing this book is an amazing gift, and I am honored by it. Thank you from the bottom of my heart for receiving these principles. I sincerely hope they change your life in some small way.

Think about what it could mean if you choose to experience gratitude at some point each day for the rest of your life. Imagine what your life would look like if you became an expert at understanding and applying the FLIP Formula. You would be far less likely to snap at your child or spouse or shake your fist at that car in front of you.

And because you would be in a different state of mind, you may offer what you think is a meaningless smile to a stranger at the exact moment he or she needs it most, instead of wearing a searing scowl that confirms to those around you that this life is not worth living.

What if that stranger was to observe your grin and wonder why you have that smile on your face, and then maybe, just maybe, a tiny one breaks across the stranger's face as well. When he or she smiles, maybe the anger or anxiety this person was feeling breaks down is replaced with a small light inside. Maybe that light lingers and causes that stranger to offer a tiny smile to another passerby.

You may think that FLIPping the Gratitude Switch during some tiny moment today won't have some sort of butterfly effect on the world… but it CAN and it WILL!!

I'm so thankful to know the simple but eternal power of gratitude.

Now the question for you is, "Do I roll the dice and see if FLIPping the Gratitude Switch changes the world for the better today and trickles a little more love and light on a sometimes dark and dreary world, or do I hoard my goodwill and stew in my stubborn selfish ways?" I hope you will join me in saying:

"Today, I choose gratitude.
Today, I choose light.
Today, I choose to do my tiny part to change the world!"

If you will do that… you will change the world. We can change the world together!

If anything in this book, even just one simple idea, has resonated as truth with you; if any part of the FLIP Formula or the concepts of *FLIP The Gratitude Switch* have benefitted and blessed you, I ask you to please share this book, and this message of the life altering power of gratitude with someone else.

Give them a copy of the book. Give them *your* copy of the book. Consider joining the FLIP movement through our private Facebook Group at **https://www.facebook.com/groups/TheFLIPMovement/**

If I may extend three brief challenges to you, I will do so with the hope that you will take me up on all of them, and that you will watch your life, and the lives of those you love most, change as a result of what you are about to do.

Challenge #1: The 30-Day Gratitude Challenge

Take The 30-Day Gratitude Challenge by visiting **kevinclayson.com/challenge**. Once there, you can register for the challenge, which is similar to the gratitude experiment that I conducted with my group of volunteers. You can track your progress and quiz scores for the 30-day period, and at the end, when you send in your scores, we'll provide you with a report showing your increased levels of happiness after you FLIPped The Gratitude Switch at least once a day for 30 days. We'll also share with you the areas of your life that most drastically changed based on your scores. Those who complete all 30 days and submit their scores will receive a special Bonus Gift. Visit

<u>kevinclayson.com/challenge</u> for rules and instructions for signing up.

Challenge #2: The #Gratifuel Challenge
This is a big one, even bigger than the last, but far easier. The #Gratifuel Challenge doesn't require you to do anything but eat a meal and have a conversation.

Here is how the challenge works: Within the next week, have a conversation about gratitude with one person. It only needs to be one conversation, and only needs to be done one time for you to complete the challenge. Share with that person an epiphany you have had about the transformative power of gratitude in your life. Then, you will ask the person to pay it forward by accepting the #Gratifuel Challenge him or herself and talk to another person about the transformative power of gratitude. I've made it simple for you. Just visit **kevinclayson.com/challenge** and print the one-page "Challenge Invitation." Give this piece of paper to the person you share your gratitude story with, and he or she will have all the instructions for how to keep paying it forward. Of course, you will also ask this person to ask another person to pay it forward and keep the challenge going.

If you will do this, we can spark a sweeping global increase in happiness levels, simply because more and more conversations about the power of gratitude will be taking place. Let's use gratitude to fuel change and happiness in the world just as it can fuel change and happiness in you.

We are going to change the world.

For more information, to watch a brief video on how to accept the #Gratifuel Challenge, and to play a part in a movement that can quite literally change the world, one simple conversation at a time, please visit: **kevinclayson.com/challenge.**

Challenge #3: The FLIP Challenge
This challenge may be the most important one of the three in terms of its ability to spread goodwill and the message of active gratitude as quickly as possible. This one we call the FLIP Challenge.

In the next 24 hours, perform the FLIP Formula at least one time, and record a quick video about what your frustration was, no matter how small that frustration was, and how you effectively used the four steps of the Formula to FLIP the Gratitude Switch and power-up with #gratifuel, then post your video on social media.

This video will serve as a marvelous bit of proof for you personally that this formula works, and will also serve as a beacon of hope to others that the Formula could work for them, too. Remember, one of the best ways to hold yourself accountable for becoming a frequent and consistent FLIPper is to share your experiences with others.

At the conclusion of your video, challenge, and tag by name, three family members or friends to complete the challenge just as you did. Even if they have yet to read this book, they will learn from your video what it looks and feels like to FLIP the Gratitude Switch, and they will be able to easily share their experience with the world, as well as challenge three additional people to do the same. You can even link them to **kevinclayson.com/challenge** where they can download the FLIP Cheat Sheet and watch a brief video on how to take and spread this challenge.

If you will do this, we can instantly spread the power and joy that can come through gratitude, and infuse the world with massive amounts of awesome right away. Use the hashtag #FLIPChallenge, and you will immediately be entered into a contest to win additional books that you can give away as gifts to those you care about or to strangers who need this message in their lives. FLIPpers of the world, unite!

One Final Message to You
the Reader, and to You, my Friend

Thank you for reading my book. Thank you for being my friend; I truly do feel like we are friends now that we've been through this journey together. Thank you for all you do. Thank you for being YOU! May God bless you and your family.

I sincerely hope to hear from you about the transformative effects of active gratitude in your life. Don't ever hesitate to reach out to me. I want to connect with you so we can change the world together.

Allow me to remind you one last time of what the power of gratitude and FLIPping the Gratitude Switch can do for you:

The simple, daily, consistent, conscious decision to enact gratitude at key strategic moments throughout the day by FLIPping the Gratitude Switch using the four-part FLIP Formula will be the single largest driver of your success, the single most important factor to your ongoing happiness, and will lead to complete fulfillment in your life.

Now get out there and start FLIPping!

Farewell for now.

With Love and Gratitude,

Kevin E. Clayson

Appendix

The #Gratifuel Action Guide:

Lessons From Patros

Coming Soon!

The follow-up book to this one is called *The #Gratifuel Action Guide*. This guide will focus on eight key areas of life where the application of the FLIP Formula will have the most profound effect.

For the #Gratifuel Action Guide, I conducted dozens of interviews with some of the most successful, extraordinary, and inspiring folks I have ever met. *The #Gratifuel Action Guide* will be a collection of their stories, and it will describe how these people have used gratitude to overcome some of the greatest challenges imaginable and go on to achieve enormous levels of success.

You have already read about the eight areas without realizing it. I included these topics in the Jacob and Patros story. Patros made some bold and powerful claims in his letter to Jacob—and in this appendix; I have included each of those claims and provided a small taste of what we will cover in *The #Gratifuel Action Guide*.

Enjoy!

Patros Claim #1
There is success embedded in every failure.

Allow me to let you in on a little secret. I don't believe in failure; I only believe that we are given stepping-stones to success. When my youngest child learned how to walk, I remember thinking that each step he took, even if he fell down, was a cause for celebration. My baby's stumbles and falls weren't failures; they were *actual steps* in the right direction. That is a type of success.

What about in business? In my company, we have developed and launched products that have flopped. Years ago, we launched what I thought was a great idea. It was an affordable membership program that would give you access to things like on-demand attorneys, dental and vision discounts, prescription discounts, and identity theft protection, to name a few perks. I thought there was no way someone would pass up on investing $40 a month in a product like that.

Well, I was absolutely wrong. No one bought it.

Ultimately, that was not a failure because we accomplished something by figuring out that no one wanted that product. That whole process moved us one step closer to developing another product that generated over $1 million dollars of revenue in its first year. We would've never developed the million-dollar idea if we hadn't fallen flat with the other.

How could we possibly look at that as a failure? It was a stepping-stone to success.

Gratitude Switch FLIPped!

Patros Claim #2
There is joy embedded in despair.

The word "embedded" means that something has been fixed to or is deeply inside something else. And I submit that you can find joy *inside* despair. Let me give you an example.

I was married for three and a half years before getting divorced at the young age of 25. I was filled with despair when my wife left me, and it hurt that she didn't want me anymore. In the instant I felt that despair, I also made the choice to feel joy for the good times we had experienced together during our brief marriage. I remembered the good, and it shifted my entire internal barometer of joy and happiness.

A friend of mine recently went through a tough break up. She truly felt that this man was going to be her husband and they would grow old together. In trying to help her deal with the hurt, I was reminded of what I learned through my divorce. I told her, "It is just a matter of time before you will feel like yourself again. This whole thing will become a footnote to a much happier time, and it will be these moments of pain that will forge your happiness in the future… I promise."

I know that to be true because *that* is what happened with me. I was filled with despair when my ex-wife announced she was leaving me and no longer loved me. Sure, I was devastated when I learned that she had fallen in love with someone else; however, in the instant I felt that despair, I also chose to feel joy for the good times we had experienced and the memories we had created. When I shifted my focus to the good parts of our relationship, it also shifted my internal barometer — and to my surprise, that internal shift is exactly what allowed me to step out of pain and into possibility.

Gratitude Switch FLIPped!

Patros Claim #3
There is hope embedded in tragedy.

Most of us have had the unfortunate experience of losing someone we love. It is a truly tragic event, which could cause you to question, "How can there be any hope embedded in tragedy?"

If you lose someone you love, you may be able to find hope in the fact that he or she has gone to a better place. I believe that when we pass from this life to the next, we go to live with our Father in Heaven. Whatever your faith, most religious traditions promote the belief that death is somehow the beginning of something new. Is there not some hope in that?

I find that any beginning contains within it a hope for something better, something exciting, and something new. I have lost grandparents who had been suffering with physical pain and mental anguish to such an extent that their bodies were no longer able to function. I feel there is hope in considering that they were able to cast off their mortality and go to a place with greener pastures, no more physical pain, and perhaps a full restoration of their once sparkling mental capacities?

I believe that part of God's plan for us is to come to this earth, experience what life offers, learn what we can, and move from this life into the next, where we are no longer bogged down by these mortal receptacles called bodies. In other words, tragedy in this life can be the opening to eternity in the life of those we tragically lose. I feel a sense of optimism and hope in that.

Gratitude Switch FLIPped!

Patros Claim #4
There is gain embedded in loss.

When Patros speaks of loss in this context, he is largely referring to the loss of a job, the loss of income, the loss of physical capabilities, the loss of our keys, or the loss of other material possessions.

How can there be any sort of "gain" with such losses?

I subscribe to the theory that when one door closes, another door somewhere has just swung open. If I lose my job, I believe that while I suffered a loss, I also gained an experience. I was able to learn what I did wrong or what I could have done better.

If we choose to believe that the loss is out of our control, then we gain the experience to look life's challenges in the eyes and learn that we get to choose the next step on the road. In many instances, if the loss can fuel our determination, what we gain on the other side of the loss far outweighs what the loss cost us.

Gratitude Switch FLIPped!

Patros Claim #5
There is opportunity embedded in hardship.

Did you know that Michael Jordan was cut from his high school basketball team as a sophomore? Most would consider this to be a devastating loss, but for Michael, it provided him with an opportunity to work harder and improve his focus and level of dedication, and as a result, cultivate the work ethic and skill set that helped him to become the greatest player who ever played professional basketball.

In his own words, "I think not making the Varsity team drove me to really work at my game, and also taught me that if you set goals and work hard to achieve them—the hard work can pay off."

Michael proves the point that if we choose to see it, if we choose to really search for the opportunity embedded in the hardship, then we can find an opportunity to get better, faster, stronger, or more efficient.

If you face some form of hardship, view it for what it is, and then take it in stride to create a different and *better* outcome as a result. If you view adversities in this way, every single hardship you encounter becomes a massive gift of opportunity and progress in your life.

Gratitude Switch FLIPped.

Patros Claim #6
There is healing embedded in pain.

The kind of Patros is referring to is not physical pain; he is talking about emotional pain. Even so, healing from emotional pain is much like the healing you can find in the process of healing from physical pain.

Take a scraped knee for example. Most of my scraped knees as a boy came from my desire to do tricks on BMX bikes. I jumped off ramps and obstacles, I tried to surf on my bike while it was moving down the street, and I tried to be like the stunt men I'd seen in my favorite movies as a kid.

As you can imagine, I experienced more than a few falls and a whole mess of scrapes, bruises and sprains. Each time I would expose the rawness under my outer layer of skin; my body would immediately go to work healing itself.

There is a universal truth embedded in our body's response to a skinned knee. The moment we experience emotional or physical pain of any kind, our bodies and minds instantly seek to start the work of healing.

The hurt may leave scars once it's healed, but scars are beautiful— they are physical or emotional representations of healing. Even more importantly, those scarring experiences and the subsequent healing are what make us who we are today. And, exactly who we are today perfectly equips us for who we will become tomorrow. All and all, pain can be viewed as the opportunity to heal, change, and become something new—and there is joy in that thought.

Gratitude Switch FLIPped!

Patros Claim #7
There is comfort embedded in chaos.

We are all our toughest critics; I know that is certainly the case for me. I have been beating myself up for years about the chaotic nature in which I work. I am quick to be distracted, and I'm quick to be the one doing the distracting.

At times, this tendency has caused a good deal of chaos in my life. It often makes me feel unable to make sense of anything. I will look around and nothing is where it's supposed to be, and it makes my mind explode from the stress of it all.

Here is how I've discovered comfort in chaos. I decided that experiencing chaos is a blessing. Chaos is an indicator that you are very much ALIVE! If you are moving from one thing to another, if you start this and get distracted and head over to do that, all of it has a quality of movement.

Movement only happens when you are alive.

If you have chaos, you are living life, and if you are witnessing chaos and are alive, then you have this amazing opportunity to clear the deck. You can choose to create organization out of the chaos because by being alive, you have the gift of choice. I find comfort in knowing that the power to change, create, and simplify is all found in the more prominent power of life.

Gratitude Switch FLIPped!

Patros Claim #8
There is a new beginning embedded in every ending.

Think of the last time something came to an end. Maybe it was a relationship, maybe it was a career, maybe it was closing the book on your child's high school or college career, or maybe it was you closing the book on your own high school or college career.

Well, I dare you to find that most recent "ending" and defend it as the real "end" to anything. I know it seems cliché, but pause for a moment and consider how profound and powerful this simple thought really is. If something just ended, then you are no longer bound to that thing, which means you can create a new story and a new adventure. There is certainly a beginning embedded in every ending, because if there wasn't, then we'd all be doomed to experiencing the same things over and over again.

And where's the fun in that?

The conclusion of one meal is the beginning of the time frame that will include your next meal. The final seconds of one game begins the preparation period for the next game. The divorce you just went through enables you to go out and find true love. The job you lost is now a new line on your resume and a collection of learned skills and experiences that will help you land the next job, or start your own company.

The next time you experience the conclusion of anything, choose to view it as the beginning of the next thing, and then feel your heart swell with the optimism that is found in unrestrained possibility.

Gratitude Switch FLIPped!

A Few Special Offers

Speaking

I've worked with people all over the country and coached business-es of all sizes, helping them learn and apply the FLIP Formula. I've spoken at company retreats, multiple-day intensive events, big corporate keynotes, and small business trainings. The results are always the same: *Happiness and productivity increases, kindness to co-workers and customers improves, and as a result, revenue increases.*

If you work for or own a small business, or large business, or work with or know of an association that could benefit from any part of this mes-sage, and you would like me to come in and speak at your company, visit: **kevinclayson.com/speaker**.

I love to speak at elementary schools, middle schools, junior high schools, high schools, charter schools, and colleges in an effort to help these institutions shift and reshape their student culture, and also to provide them with a catalyst for improving grades, breeding leaders, and overcoming bul-lying. The up and coming generations need to have their minds awakened to what life can look like, and they need to know that they already have within them the ability to overcome peer pressure and depression, and achieve true success (whatever that success looks like for them). I can always tailor my message for the specific needs of an organization, and I would love to do that for your students or your school.

I've spoken at churches and other religious organizations, and if there is any way I could possibly serve, entertain, or simply bring a little color and joy to your organization, your school, your company, your asso-ciation, or your church group, feel free to download my speaking packets. They are free, and they are awesome, and I put them together for YOU!!

Again, just visit **kevinclayson.com/speaker** for a free speaker's kit to see what I can offer you and your audience. I guarantee we can work within the budget you have, and I can even show you how to have me come and speak to your group for free.

Work With Me

If you would like some one-on-one time with me, I have coaching and mentoring opportunities available for a limited number of people. I can only take on one or two students a month for personal coaching, and while I will consider everyone, I will not accept everyone. We also have an entire Membership Community that gives you every tool you need to become a consistent and frequent FLIPper. The Community will also give you con-sistent access to me, and to an entire community dedicated to FLIPping The Gratitude Switch and the FLIP Formula. I can guarantee that an investment yourself, and in your access to the #Gratifuel Community will change your life and the lives of those around you in a measurable and valuable way.

Visit: **kevinclayson.com/coaching** to get more information and to find out how you can try out the Community with absolutely zero risk.

SPECIAL OFFERS

Acknowledgements

There are so many people who have contributed to my life, and to my ability to write this book. I'm sure I will forget many who've had an impact, and for that I'm sorry. This book is a huge part of my life's work and all of you helped me get to this point.

First off, all of my gratitude goes to my Heavenly Father, His Son Jesus Christ, and my constant companion, the Holy Ghost, without whom none of this would have even been possible. The thoughts, and ideas that make up this book, as well as my ability to be able to put it all together, would have never been possible were it not for my Creator and His eternal, and perfect plan of happiness, and for the Gospel of Jesus Christ.

To my amazing wife Malana. I get choked up at the mere thought of all that you have had to endure as we've been on this roller coaster of life, and the thrill ride of writing and publishing this book. You amaze me with your unwavering support, your unconditional love, and your constant encouragement. This book would not have been possible without you. You are my greatest partner, and my greatest idea sounding board. You offered so many amazing and game changing ideas, that this book would look far different were it not for you, for your genius, and for your love and belief in this message. Thank you for believing in the message enough to adopt it and teach it to our children. I don't know if I am a good man, but if I am, or ever resemble one, it will be because of who I have become through loving you. You are my hero, and my best friend, and my one and only EC. I love you; I love you, I LOVE YOU!!!!

To my kids Brooklyn, Braxton, and Brody. You are my best friends, my greatest teachers, and the reason I get up every day and try to do something good in this life. You drive me and fuel me more than I can ever articulate. I love you; I love you, I LOVE YOU!!!

Brooklyn, you are the first one that taught me how simple FLIPping the Gratitude Switch really was, as I watched you begin to apply it as a beautiful little 5-year-old. Now, years later, I have continued to enjoy watching you use it to give you perspective and smiles, even when it feels hard to be thankful. I love you! Thank you for your example my sweetheart!

Braxton, you are the first one that showed me the sheer joy that could be found in FLIPping the Gratitude Switch as you jumped around on our trampoline, happily singing the "FLIP the Gratitude Switch" song you made up. I love you! Thank you my buddy-boy!

Brody, the sparkle in your eyes, and the light in your smile have been the perfect example of pure joy that I've always hoped to bottle up, and even partially communicate to others through the words in this book. I love you! Thank you for flooding my life with joy too!

To my parents, Kendall and Sharon Clayson. You have endured financial sacrifice, and consistent uncertainty as you supported me for so many years in my attempt to do something great with my life. You have never doubted me, and your continuous belief in who I could become, often times when I offered you no real proof that I could be someone worth believing in, have always amazed me. Your examples of kindness and service in this life have stood as constant reminders of what it means to be good, and to live a Christ-like life. I love you, and thank you!

To my in-laws, Doug and Janet Hunt. You have been the best cheerleaders I could ask for. You made our family FLIP The Gratitude Switch t-shirts for us all to wear, long before I had even thought about FLIP shirts. You read my early drafts with care, and traveled hundreds of miles to watch me speak as I was starting to spread this message. For a man who is only related to you by marriage, you have treated me better than blood, and for that I am eternally grateful. I love you, and thank you!

My beloved Wilson Clan, Kristen, Russell, Katelyn, Brayden, Lexie, and Brynlee. You guys have been my rocks. You gave me a home when I needed one. You took Malana in as family before she ever was. You have given me endless hours of joy and laughter. Thanks for being some of my best friends and greatest supports ever. My gratitude for you is deep. I love you and thank you!

A special thank you to all of the Hunt and Davies side of the family for your love and support! Melanie and Chris Elder, Brian and Angie Hunt, Shaun and Michelle Hunt, Kendell and Jackie Hunt, Brett and Erica Hunt, Marie, Chalyce, Colby, and Chay Carter, Steve Hunt, MaRee Farnsworth, Joe and Jeff Hunt and your amazing wives Ashley and Terra, Josh and Callie Crum, and to all our amazing nieces and nephews, Kyler and Bekah Hunt, Erica and Nate Smith, Logan, Jordan, Justin, Dallin, Danielle, Jared, Mallory, Whitney, Katie, Gage, Colton, Madee, Saydie, Ethan, Bailee, and Ian and Corben… thank you all!

Kris Krohn and Steve Earl. Thank you for giving me space to create my life's work, and for believing in me for so many years. Because of the company we had, I was given countless opportunities to learn how to speak, and learn how to be in business. Thank you for the many lessons and, for the decades of friendship and support.

A special thank you to Tyler and Leigh Bennett and Amara Day Spa and Salon. You guys believed in my value as a paid speaker long before I did. The amazing opportunities you gave me to speak to, train, and entertain your amazing staff and company, are some of my treasured memories. Thank you for constantly believing in me. With all your help and support, I might actually do something worthwhile with my life beyond being the poster child for male nose hair waxing. Thank you.

Another special thank you to Stephen and Anne Miller. You two are some of the best friends a guy could ever ask for. Anne and Stephen, you two have helped me believe in myself, and that is truly a gift of tremendous value. Stephen, I can't even begin to tally up the minutes and hours spent bouncing ideas off one another, and taking time to discuss what really matters in life. You are my beat boxing brother, and a true and eternal friend. Thank you.

Thank you to my good friend Anthony Andelin who believed in *FLIP the Gratitude Switch* and in my ability to motivate and move an audience. So much of my skill set was honed because of the events we did together. You have acted as vital counsel to me, and as a true friend and at times a much needed mentor. Thank you!

A huge thank you to James Malinchak. You acted as my coach, mentor and friend for two of the most important years of my life, and even before we worked together directly, it was your seminar that created the space for me to learn some of the most vital truths in success. Your recommendation to take *FLIP the Gratitude Switch,* and to turn it into a simple and digestible formula was such a game changer, and truly helped me understand even more than I had, the power of what it was I was doing in my life that I felt compelled to share with the world. Thank you!

Thank you to Hal Elrod, because without the miracle morning I never would have found the time to make this happen. You continue to be a source of inspiration for me, and I'm so thankful above all to have your friendship. Thank you for writing the forward to this book, and being a success story I can aspire to be like. Thank you!

Thank you to my friend Bob Burg for showing me how to write a business book that can have a global impact. Thank you for being a constant example of what you teach. Never has a business book had a greater effect on me than *The Go-Giver.* The principles in your book have literally charted a new course for my entire life. And, of course John David Mann who's contribution to the book *The Go-Giver* is also part of the life changing experience that has taken place for me. Thank you!

Thank you to Don and Heidi Childs for believing in me and in the message. Thank you for being an integral part of this book's ability to see the light of day. Your incredible generosity has touched Malana and me so deeply, and

I truly believe that your investment in me and in this message will pay temporal and eternal dividends. Thank you!

Thank you to one of my heroes, President Dieter F. Uchtdorf. Thank you for your awe inspiring commitment to teaching the Gospel of Jesus Christ. You have taught me more than I can say. After I began the journey of learning and teaching gratitude, your talk "Grateful in Any Circumstances," was a confirmation to me of the importance of this work and these teachings. What you said in that talk changed my perspective, and became a huge foundation for my belief in the importance of writing this book, and through the Spirit, because of your words, I gained a greater understanding of the very topic I felt called to teach. Recht vielen Dank mein Bruder.

Thank you to another one of my heroes, Glenn Beck. It may seem unconventional to thank a TV and radio host but you have become much more to me than that. Although we have only met briefly, you influence my life for good every day. You are one of my heroes, and your commitment to principles, to truth, and to sharing that truth no matter what the cost, is a huge inspiration to me, and has continued to fuel me during the creation of this book. Thank you Glenn! I sincerely hope one day to break bread with you, and simply express the impact you have had on my life through your example.

Thank you to Glenn Morshower for your unwavering commitment to being you! For a long time I stopped dancing on stage. I was worried it wasn't professional enough. Then I saw you dance on stage and I went back to just being me, and that single decision has brought me such joy and contentment, and frankly a little notoriety. Thank you!

Thank you to my amazing ghost writer, Jennifer Lill Brown for being the most incredible ghost writer in the world. Thank you for keeping my soul in this book, and for sharing with me, and the readers, that this book changed your life as you worked on it. You helped me believe in me, and in this message. We became friends along the way and although you bit off more than you could chew with my indecision and constant evolution, I sincerely hope that it will pay you back many times over in some way. Thank you for taking my unpolished, albeit important and powerful gibberish (wink), and polishing it into one of the things I will be most proud of accomplishing in my entire life. One of your greatest accomplishments was turning my endless use of the exclamation point into equally exciting sentences with mere periods. Thank you Ms. J. Kittenstreet!

John Lee Dumas, thank you for interviewing me twice on your amazing podcast, and for being the first to let me share FLIPping the Gratitude Switch to a large audience. In many ways the success of this movement can be traced back to you, your kindness, and to Fire Nation. Thank you!

ACKNOWLEDGEMENTS

Thank you to all the other amazing podcast hosts who have featured me and this message, and given me time with your precious audiences to share this simple formula, and thank you to those of you that gave me your stage as well. To Rob Shallenberger, Dr. Paul Jenkins, Jason Klop, Leigh Martinuzzi, Adam Shankman, Jason Klop, Nicholas and Amanda Bayerle, Brandie Weikle, Kimberly Snyder, Ted Prodromou, M.C. Laubscher, Geoff Woods, Charlie Poznek, Matt Remuzzi, Matthew and Bonnie Parks, Doug Gulbrandsen, Michael and Debbye Cannon, Patrick Donohoe, Mike Deblis, Julie Hatch, Jennifer and Cole Pack, Mariah Haws, Heather Brown, Anna Seewald, and of course Chris Miles.

To my sports heroes, Steve Young, Joe Theismann, Stephen Curry, and James "Iron Cowboy" Lawrence, thank you for being examples of excellence and inspiration in every way.

To my motivational heroes, Zig Ziglar, Jim Rohn, Wayne Dyer, Walt Disney, Steve Jobs, Les Brown, Brian Tracy, Jack Canfield, Dan Clark, and my good friend Greg S. Reid, thank you for proving to me that this world can be changed one talk at a time.

A double thank you to Greg S. Reid for writing a book that I absolutely needed during my darkest hour of creating this one. *Three Feet From Gold* taught me that success was both possible and frankly inevitable when you follow your heart and that burning desire within.

To the best dance crew on the planet, The Jabbawockeez, thank you for providing me much needed inspiration any time I opened YouTube or went to your shows. Your commitment to your craft made me more committed to mine. #WockAsOne

To the members of Pentatonix, thank you for bringing a smile to my face, chills to my arms, and impromptu dance parties to my family. You guys make me believe I can be something worth being no matter where I may start from!

To Rob Van Winkle AKA Vanilla Ice, your graciousness and support when we met, meant the world!! Thanks for letting me perform your song to bring smiles to the youth I speak to and entertain. My wife also reluctantly thanks you, since I performed your song at our wedding. Thanks for writing and creating a song that has been my companion, and a burst of energy for me for over 20 years!

To my heroes in book writing and inspiration, thank you! Each of your books, and your examples, have touched me deeply, taught me much, and made me a better me. To Darren Hardy, Marcus, Lemonis, John Assaraf, Simon Sinek, Dave Blanchard, Adam M. Grant, Ph.D., John C. Maxwell, Tony

Hsieh, Grant Cardone, MJ Demarco, Seth Godin, Sally Hogshead, Patrick Lencioni, Malcolm Gladwell, Michael Hyatt, Gay Hendricks, Craig Duswalt, Dr. Paul Jenkins, Rob Shallenberger, Peter Voogd, David Bach, Byron Katie, Greg McKeown, Sharon Lechter, Tim Ferriss, Lisa Nichols, Jon Huntsman Sr., Barbara Corcoran, Kevin Harrington, Bruce C. Lipton, Dev Patnaik, Gary Vaynerchuk, Michael E. Gerber, Jim Collins, Daymond John, Jeff Olson, Michael Port, Jon Acuff, Gregg Braden, Eckhart Tolle, Robert Kiyosaki, Sean Stephenson, Walter Isaacson, Gary Chapman, T. Harv Eker, David M. McCullough, Mitt Romney, Wallace D. Wattles, Dale Carnegie, Og Mandino, Napoleon Hill, The Napoleon Hill Foundation, Ayn Rand, Paulo Coelho, Thomas J. Stanley, Leslie Householder, and Kip Tindell… thank you!!

To my good friends, and my constant foundation of support, thank you all for what you mean to me, and what you continue to do for me. I am a better man for knowing each of you, and you are all heroes of mine in one way or another. Each of you has had an influence on this book, although many of you don't even realize the impact you have made on me and this message, but THANK YOU! In no particular order, thank you to John Moyer, Sydney King, Garen Winn, Thomas Blackwell, Kevin Eastman, Rich German, Corey Shanes, Rachel Maser, Ryan Whetten, Sherry Winn, Lavonna Roth, Cat Crews, Mike and LeAnn Fritz, Matt Jones, Timothy Benson, Mike Tomasello, Mike Driggers and Gaby Lopez-Aguilera, Nick Peterson, Mark and Kaylinn Morrell, Tiana Von Johnson, Lola Thompson, Becky Sampson, Heather Madder, Kristi Frank, Dan Gheesling, Thurl "Big T" Bailey, Keefe Duarte, Matt Theriault, Sharon Wahlig, Greg Blackbourn, Cindy McLane, Davy Tyburski, Carson Tjietjen, Gary and Carolyn Norris, Julia Zacharias, Trent S. White, Patrick Manning, Jason Manning, Robin Romero, Christa Burneff, Sharla Mandere, Tisa Penny, Sheila Homer, Joe Herrera, Trisha and Craig Dixon, Deby Bauer, Wylene and Clint Benson, Crichton Uale, Celeste Johnson, Leslie Johnson, Michelle and Alan Wright, Dr. Alberto Alexander, Susan Bond, Hans Helmuth, Stephen Caruthers, Lauren Bachmann, Teresa R. Martin, Kevin Young, Joel Stewart, Jimmy Rex, Peter and Marie Glahn, Brent Rose, Benjamin and Miriam Hougue, Janicey Morneau, Tracy and LaVieve Roberts, Joseph Roberts, Kelli Naylor, Kristen and Riley Alexander, Robert Michael Sester, Gerry Heaton, Ryan Whetten, Rick Titan, John Peterson, Kevin Mohler, Travis J. Brown, Brad and Karen Trunell, Blake Butcher, Al Harris, Cheryl Buckley, David Keyser, Clint and Stefani Severson, TW Walker and Heather O'Brian, Angela Walters, April Nelson, Scott Hammerle, Julie Marie Carrier, Nick Hoyer, Stephanie Lee, Annabelle Lee, Greg Hudnall, Gabe and Annabella Cruz, Val Hale, Teresa Souza, Pat Schultz, Roy Mayeda, Jim Clark, Rodney White, Keith Burnett, Evan Money, Tommy Schaff, Curtiss Murphy, Stephen and Karina Palmer, David Kirlew, Eric Jeandebien, Eric and Julie Gurr, Jon Malgradi, Kendal Blunck, Dusty Dastrup, Sharon Whalig, Chad Wade, Justin Yates, Ryan Jaten, Nathan Hall, James and Marianne Shuman, McKay and Danielle Matheson, Ken and Marlene Matheson, Marty Matheson, Shanon Brooks, Dustin Christensen, Carl and

ACKNOWLEDGEMENTS

Cindy Tiede, Todd Kiser, Steffi Meyne, Brandon Grange, Sue Smith, Josh Smith, Curt Cummings, Robyn Wilson, Jennifer Jewell, Kristen Russo, Ben and Susan Booth, and so many more... THANK YOU ALL!

Thank you to my many spiritual advisors over the years who have had a profound impact on my life. August Schubert, Jay Pimentel, Ben Beeson, Brent Webb, Mike Danielson Sr., McKay Matthews, Gary Baker, John Bytheway, Gordon B. Hinckley, Thomas. S. Monson, Jeffrey R. Holland, Ezra Taft Benson, David A. Bednar, Neal A. Maxwell, and many more; thank you for helping to show me where to find my Father in Heaven!

To my marketing masters and examples, Russell Brunson, James Malinchak, Dan Kennedy, Joe Polish, Jeff Walker, Arthur Tubman, Chandler Bolt, Clate Mask, Ryan Deiss, Brent Attaway, Scott Marshall, and Tim Grahl. Thank you for helping this book see the light of day and reach those who can be blessed by it.

And of course to YOU the reader. Thank you for reading this book!

Notes

Preface

1. Melody Beattie, *Pass It On, Values.com,* http://www.values.com/inspirational-quotes/7164-gratitude-unlocks-the-fullness-of-life-it

2. David A. Bednar, LDS General Conference, "The Windows of Heaven," (October 2013), https://www.lds.org/general-conference/2013/10/the-windows-of-heaven?lang=eng&_r=1

Part 2, Chapter 3

1. Dieter F. Uchtdorf, LDS General Conference, "Grateful in Any Circumstances," (April 2014), https://www.lds.org/general-conference/2014/04/grateful-in-any-circumstances?lang=eng&_r=1

Part 2, Chapter 4

1. The Harris Poll, "Are You Happy? It May Depend on Age, Race/Ethnicity and Other Factors," (May 30, 2013), http://www.theharrispoll.com/health-and-life/Are_You_Happy__It_May_Depend_on_Age__Race_Ethnicity_and_Other_Factors.html

2. Alfred D. Souza, *Pass It On, Values.com,* http://www.values.com/inspirational-quotes/5094-for-a-long-time-it-had-seemed-to-me-that-life

3. Joseph B. Wirthlin, Devotional Address Given At Brigham Young University, "Live in Thanksgiving Daily," (October 31, 2000), Published September 2001 in *The Ensign,* https://www.lds.org/ensign/2001/09/live-in-thanksgiving-daily?lang=eng

Part 3, Chapter 2

1. Corrie Ten Boom, *The Hiding Place* (Bantam Books; Reprint edition, 1974).

Part 3, Chapter 3

1. John Assaraf story, *The Secret,* Director Drew Heriot. Prime Time Productions, 2006. Film.

Part 3, Chapter 4

1. Vaughan Bell, "The Unsexy Truth About Dopamine," *The Guardian* (February 2, 2013), https://www.theguardian.com/science/2013/feb/03/dopamine-the-unsexy-truth

2. Sinek, Simon. *Leaders Eat Last: Why Some Teams Pull Together and Others Don't.* Portfolio/Penguin, 2014. Print.

3. Korb, Alex, Ph. D. "The Grateful Brain: The Neuroscience of Giving Thanks." *Psychology Today,* November 20, 2012. https://www.psychologytoday.com/blog/prefrontal-nudity/201211/the-grateful-brain

Kevin's Favorite Books

A Quick List of Books That Will Change Your Life and Your Business

1. *The Go-Giver* by Bob Burg and John David Mann

2. *The Miracle Morning* by Hal Elrod

3. *The Science of Getting Rich* by Wallace D. Wattles

4. *Think and Grow Rich* by Napoleon Hill

5. *How To Win Friends & Influence People* by Dale Carnegie

6. *The Greatest Salesman In The World* by Og Mandino

7. *Give and Take: Why Helping Others Drives Our Success* by Adam M. Grant

8. *The Big Leap* by Gay Hendricks

9. *The Slight Edge* by Jeff Olson

10. *Winners Never Cheat* by Jon Huntsman Sr.

11. *The Compound Effect* by Darren Hardy

12. *Wired To Care* by Dev Patnaik

13. *Essentialism* by Greg McKeown

14. *Three Feet From Gold* by Greg S. Reid and Sharon Lechter

15. *Start With Why* by Simon Sinek

Tell Me About Your FLIP's

Twitter: @kevinclayson (Tag your tweet with #gratifuel)

Facebook: Facebook.com/KevinClaysonCOOA

Instagram: Kevin Clayson

Facebook Book Page: Facebook.com/gratifuel

Group Page: Facebook.com/groups/TheFLIPMovement/

LinkedIn: Linkedin.com/in/kevin-clayson-10881a11

Blog: gratifuel.com

Email: kevin@kevinclayson.com

Made in USA - North Chelmsford, MA
1054477_9781537208244
03.18.2020 0840